Mystical Verses of Lallā

A Journey of Self Realization

Translated with an Introduction by
JAISHREE KAK

Illustrations by
JOSEPH SINGER

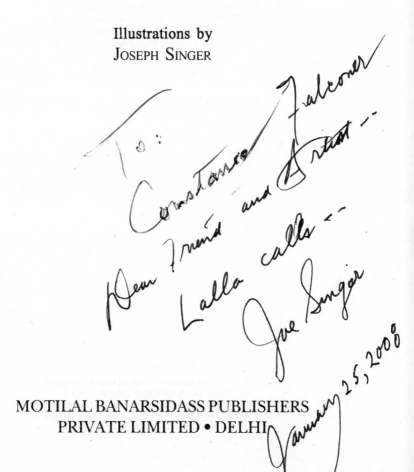

To:
Constance Falconer
Dear Friend and Artist --
Lalla calls --
Joe Singer
January 25, 2000

MOTILAL BANARSIDASS PUBLISHERS
PRIVATE LIMITED • DELHI

First Edition : Delhi, 2007

ISBN: 978-81-208-3255-8

MOTILAL BANARSIDASS

41 U.A. Bungalow Road, Jawahar Nagar, Delhi 110 007
8 Mahalaxmi Chamber, 22 Bhulabhai Desai Road, Mumbai 400 026
203 Royapettah High Road, Mylapore, Chennai 600 004
236, 9th Main III Block, Jayanagar, Bangalore 560 011
Sanas Plaza, 1302 Baji Rao Road, Pune 411 002
8 Camac Street, Kolkata 700 017
Ashok Rajpath, Patna 800 004
Chowk, Varanasi 221 001

PRINTED IN INDIA
BY JAINENDRA PRAKASH JAIN AT SHRI JAINENDRA PRESS,
A-45 NARAINA, PHASE-I, NEW DELHI 110 028
AND PUBLISHED BY NARENDRA PRAKASH JAIN FOR
MOTILAL BANARSIDASS PUBLISHERS PRIVATE LIMITED,
BUNGALOW ROAD, DELHI 110 007

for vajrapani

Table of Contents

Preface

Growing up in Kashmīr, I have memories of spectacular Himalayan mountains, magnificent lakes, and countless rivers snaking through the valley, and accompanying all is the echoing on festive occasions of the melodious singing of Lallā's verse-sayings, popularly known as *Lalla-Vākh*. Her outpourings are timeless and people of all faiths have treasured them. The oral transmission for centuries illustrates the extent to which she has been a part of folk memory. My old aunts who grew up in Kashmīr have memories of women reciting Lallā's verses while they spun fine shawls at the spinning wheel. Over the centuries, Lallā became the wise woman of Kashmīrī culture. She was invoked not only at moments of personal dilemma but also to celebrate moments of social togetherness. I myself remember my mother singing Lallā's verses and occasionally quoting them in her conversations.

Lallā's verses provide a revealing glimpse into her life, serving as a vehicle for the reader to participate in her most profound spiritual and emotional experiences. Her entire oeuvre presents different stages of her journey to achieve mystic communion with her higher Self or Śiva. Some of her verses deal with the early stages of her quest as she prepares her mind and body for a long and arduous journey through the inner landscape of mind. Others describe the advanced stages of her practice with sustained introspective contemplation, and yet others are uttered in the form of teachings to her community. Lallā's most profound verses are unmediated visions as she pours out her experiences into words.

Each verse, consisting of four lines, usually stands as an independent unit, though some are written as questions and answers. In translating verses, I have followed the originals as closely as possible in order to retain the spirit of Lallā's verses. I have tried to reproduce into translated language the inner form and rhythm of the originals in Kashmīrī, as I see them, by playing with punctuations, phrase breaks and line breaks. Accordingly, even though each original verse is four lines long, some of the translated verses are longer. The original Kashmīrī verse in Devanāgarī script accompanies each translated verse.

The present collection is a revised translation of the verses published in *To the Other Shore*, a critical study of Lallā's life and verses. This volume has been specifically prepared for different types of readers, especially the non-specialist. The readers interested only in Lallā's poetic outpourings have the English translations. Those proficient in the Kashmīrī language can read the English translations with the orginals in Kashmīrī. A key to pronunciation of Kashmīrī written in Devanāgarī script is provided for such readers. The collection also comes with a concordance of verses in various Lallā collections toward the end of the volume. For readers who wish to explore the Kashmīrī Śaiva philosophy that permeates Lallā's verses, a basic introduction to this thought system and its relevance to Lallā's verses is given in the appendix.

The preparation of this collection of verses has been a long journey, which started decades ago in Kashmīr when I had the good fortune of meeting the late Kashmīrī Śaiva scholar and teacher Swami Lakshman Jee. He ignited the spark. Many years later, the spark blossomed into a deep desire to work on Lallā's verses, which became an anchor around which my study of the Kashmīrī Śaiva tradition took shape. In this endevour, I acknowledge the support of my family and friends, both old and new. I owe a special gratitude to my late father Ram Nath Kak who went over my translation of the verses and shared with me his unique knowledge of the Śaiva tradition. This project would have been inconceivable without my mother Sarojini Kak who told me fascinating stories and legends about Lallā as I was growing up in Kashmīr.

I especially feel honored by the contribution of Joseph Singer, an artist, photographer and printmaker. Singer brings to life essential themes of Lallā's life and poetry as he pours her vision into illustrations. His prints and drawings complement the verses, even entering into a conversation with them, thus providing visual pathways into the verses. Singer weaves a bridge between western and eastern sensibilities by translating the verses into a contemporary visual medium. Finally, I acknowledge the continuous support of my dear friend and colleague Kathy Phillips as she went over each verse with me to see if the original Kashmīrī verse was translated in the best possible way within the constraints imposed by another language and another culture. She has my warm thanks.

Introduction

The fourteenth-century mystic poet Lallā, also known as Lalleśvarī and Lal Dĕd, is an integral part of Kashmīrī language, literature, and culture. *Lalla-Vākh*[1] or Lallā's verse-sayings have resonated orally for centuries in the valley of Kashmīr. Lallā has been compared to Shakespeare, Hafiz, Kabir and Tulsidasa. And, she has been honored as the first Kashmīrī poet who modernized Kashmīrī language as well as literature. Her richness of language, turn of phrases, and metaphors are now standard expressions in modern Kashmīrī.

Lalla-Vākh: The Text

Lallā's compositions come to us in a form that is fairly modern, except for occasional archaic expressions with obscure or unknown meaning. As is common with the prolonged transmission of any oral tradition, it is hard to imagine that her verses have come to us in this century without any change. However, the interpolations and changes were probably minimal because of a very strong oral tradition in medieval Kashmīr where some families specialized in rote memorization of texts passed on from teacher to disciple, or within the family from one generation to another. One such oral recension by an old Brāhmin Dharmadāsa Darwēsh of the village Gush in Kashmīr, was used as the basis of the first scholarly collection of Lallā's verses in the West, which was put together in 1920 by Sir

---

[1] The Kashmīrī word "vākh" is the same as the Sanskrit word "vākya." In Kashmīrī "vākh" is used both as singular as well as plural. The literal meaning of the term *Lalla-Vākh* is Lallā's Verse-Sayings.

George Grierson and Lionell D. Barnett. Dharmadāsa
Darwēsh recited Lallā's verses as he had learned them from
his elders as part of the family tradition. In addition to this
collection, Grierson consulted two other manuscripts of the
Stein collection at the Oxford Indian Institute, Stein A and
Stein B, both written in Śāradā alphabet of Kashmīrī. Since
it has not been possible to date the manuscripts that Grierson
and Barnett used, it has yet to be determined how long the
transmission of Lallā's poetry was exclusively oral.

Aside from Grierson and Barnett's 109-verse collection
published as *Lallā Vākyāni*, Pandit Anand Koul collected
seventy-five verses, which were published in the *Indian
Antiquary* in the 1930s. Quite a few in Anand Koul's
collection appear to be either variants or later additions. Some
other noteworthy collections are S. N. Charagi's *The Wise
Sayings of Laleshwari* (1938) and the special *Koshur
Samāchār* (1971) edition on Lallā. The latter is a compilation
from several different sources, but here, too, a great number
of verses can easily be rejected since they do not conform to
the style or thought content that has come to be associated
with Lallā. Other more recent collections are primarily based
on the above works.

Jayalal Kaul's study of Persian sources sheds further light
on the confusion related to some verses, since they seem to
have been mixed up with those of the Sūfī mystic Sheikh
Nūr-ud-dīn (also known as Nund Ṛṣi), a junior
contemporary of Lallā, who greatly revered her. Kaul notes
that thirty-five verses in various Lallā collections are also part
of *Nūrnāma-s* and *Ṛṣīnāma-s*, the biographies of Sheikh
Nūr-ud-dīn. Many of these verses in later copies of the
Ṛṣīnāma-s have been wrongly attributed to Sheikh Nūr-ud-
dīn, even though this mixing-up of verses is not present in
the earlier copies (Kaul 32-33). Since no concrete evidence
is available to show whether the Lallā manuscripts or copies
of manuscripts, the basis of the Grierson collection, were
written before or after the earliest *Nūrnāma* recorded two
hundred years after Sheikh Nūr-ud-dīn's death, it is difficult

to determine the true originator of the handful of verses that have been attributed both to Nūr-ud-dīn and Lallā. Ultimately, it is the style of the verses that determines their validity as hers.

The fact that Lallā's old Kashmīrī verses have come to us in a modern form intelligible to any average Kashmīrī is evidence in itself of continuing oral transmission over a fairly long period of time. It has been speculated that her verses over the centuries began to be sung by village minstrels. Later, they became part of Kashmīrī classical music (*sūfiānā kalām*) as they were sung as sacred invocations to open the assembly of Sūfīs (*Majlis-e-m'ārifīn*). Even though the language of the verses changed slowly along with the Kashmīrī language, the thought content, images, and metaphors seem to have remained the same, which gives the body of Lallā's compositions inner coherence. Her unique use of vivid concrete images and metaphors can be used as a helpful criterion for judging whether a particular verse can be attributed to her.

Life and Legends

Fourteenth century Kashmīr was a region in turmoil. The golden age of Kashmīr with its great and original contributions to literature, philosophy, drama, sculpture, painting, and architecture had passed, as the state collapsed from outside invasions and political upheavals from within. With the old order in disarray, the majority of people were concerned mainly with survival.

Queen Kotā, the last Hindu ruler of Kashmīr, actively participated in running the administration in the first few decades of the century in various capacities, including briefly as sovereign herself. Shah Mīr, a Muslim minister in the court, planned a rebellion in which she died. Kotā's death marks the end of old Kashmīr. Shah Mīr ascended the throne as Sultan Shams-ud-dīn in 1339 and started the Sultan dynasty, which ruled Kashmīr for over two centuries. The Hindu rule had been marked by religious tolerance, which continued under the early Muslim Sultans.

Lallā was born into a Brahmin family either in
Pāndrenthan or Sempor in Kashmīr sometime in the early
1300s, and she died in the 1370s. A great deal of controversy
exists as to when exactly she was born. Pandit Anand Koul
gives the date of her birth, without citing his sources, as the
middle of the fourteenth century (Koul 1921, 302). Jayalal
Kaul's study of Persian sources shows, however, that Lallā
in fact was born somewhere between 1317 and 1320, even
as early as 1300-1301. This would explain the time frame in
the first reference to Lallā in a Persian chronicle, *Wāqi'āti
Kashmīr* (1746) that describes her as having flourished or
become famous during the reign of Sultan Alāu-ud-dīn
(1343-54) and having died during the reign of Sultan
Shihāb-ud-dīn (1354-73) (Kaul pp. 5-7).

She was given in marriage to Nica Bhatta of Pāmpor at a
young age where she received a new name Padmāvatī. In
her verses, Lallā always refers to herself by her maiden name
"Lallā" and it is this name that one can with certainty say
belonged to her. In folk memory she appears with two other
names—Lalleśvarī and Lal Děd. In Persian chronicles she is
called Lallā 'Ārifa.

Legends about Lallā abound. We encounter several
images: a gentle, introspective woman; a wandering ascetic
who defies all conventions as she forges her own path; and a
spiritual teacher who offers words of wisdom with love to her
people (and to us today). Her married life was unhappy due
to her mother-in-law's harsh treatment and her husband's
angry disposition toward her. Lallā was not given enough to
eat. Her mother-in-law would serve her a stone, covered with
a thin layer of rice so as to make the serving seem large. She
would quietly eat whatever she was served without any protest.
In one legend, to prepare for a special *grahaśānti* ceremony
at her home, she goes out to fetch water from the river. One
of her neighbors teases her, saying she would have a great
feast that night. Lallā's reply—whether a lamb or a sheep is
killed at her house, the daughter-in-law will always get a
stone—has become a famous saying in Kashmīrī.

All legends agree that she was introspective and did not show a great deal of interest in worldly affairs. She is drawn early to spiritual quest. Siddha Śrīkaṇtha initiates her into the Śaiva yoga. According to a legend, Lallā walks to the nearby river in Zinypor village before dawn every day to fetch a pitcher of water as was the custom in those days. But instead of directly filling the pitcher and returning home, she crosses the river to visit the shrine of Naṭa Keśava Bhairava. Suspecting her of infidelity, her husband quietly follows her one day on her morning ritual. He finds her sitting alone by the riverbank meditating. Enraged at what he sees, he goes home. As she returns with the water pitcher on her head, he confronts her angrily about her diversion and smashes the pitcher with a stick. Even though the pitcher breaks, the legend says, the water stays miraculously intact on her head. Lallā calmly goes inside the house, and pours the water into smaller vessels until all are full. She takes the leftover water and throws it outside where a pond is formed. Later on, the pond is named "Lalla- trāg" (the Pond of Lallā) which is said to have been full of water for many centuries. The incident marks the time of her renunciation when she leaves her home and family and becomes a wandering ascetic.

Lallā's verses reveal her to be a woman with feelings, thoughts and desires. She suffers trials and tribulations that a woman in medieval society might face because she is daring to seek her own path. Some of her verses reflect her awareness of the social construction of gender, perhaps not in the same way as a contemporary woman might, but nonetheless it is an amazing insight for a woman from the medieval period. In one verse she says she came to the world like a blooming cotton flower with all potential and possibilities intact, full of enthusiasm and aspiration. However, the ginner and the carder of society reduced her to a miserable state and turned her into utility-directed fine yarn, to be hung on the weaver's loom and turned into cloth. Her social self is thus a creation of others to be put in service for others.

I, Lallā, set out hoping to bloom
like a cotton flower.
The ginner and the carder gave me hard blows.
After the spinner spun me into fine yarn,
I was stretched on the loom
in the weaver's shop. (V 13)

When the washerman dashed me on a slab of stone,
rubbing me with much soap and washing soda.
and the tailor cut me into bits with scissors,
I, Lallā, attained supreme bliss. (V 14)

Lallā feels the need to transcend the conditioning which
confines her to socially prescribed gender roles. She compares
setting herself free from this conditioning to cleaning a piece
of cloth by rubbing it with soap and dashing it on a slab of
stone to loosen the extraneous matter sticking to it. She
describes the shredding of the old identity in terms of the
washed cloth being cut into little bits by the tailor's scissors.
The "washerman" in the above verse is the self within her
that aspires to higher states of awareness and hence, engages
in acts that enable Lallā to transcend the socially defined
"feminine" self, which she experiences as oppressive. As the
tailor cuts the washed piece of cloth into bits, Lallā the
daughter, Lallā the daughter-in-law, and Lallā the wife are
torn into shreds and her true identity emerges into the open.
The "tailor" is her higher Self, which guides her to forge a
new identity that is not confined to socially prescribed modes
of behavior.

Lallā's refusal to perform the female gender role is
illustrated by the legends that describe her roaming in a nude
state after she renounces her family. Such legends are based
on the following verse:

My guru gave me only one advice—
from outside transfer the attention within.
That became Lallā's initiation—
that is why I began to wander naked. (V 50)

Lallā's wandering naked could refer to her divesting or disrobing herself of all worldly attachments, including her family, friends, and the comfort of a home. This interpretation is in line with the content of her other verses, which use a great many analogies and metaphors to convey esoteric ideas and experiences.

If we compare Lallā to another medieval Indian mystic poet/singer Mīrābāi (b. 1498), it is obvious that Lallā is more radical and challenges the patriarchal social norms at a deeper level. She rejects traditionally defined attributes of feminine self-effacement, often accompanied by devotional and supplicant approach toward spiritual experience. She takes control of her experience as a self-contained subjectivity, identifying more with Śiva than with Śakti.[2] This approach is associated with extreme austerities, self-containment, and self-absorption. No wonder her chosen deity is Śiva, the ascetic god of the Śaiva tradition.

Lallā is aware of her isolation not only in the secular world which she has renounced, but also in the spiritual world where, as an outsider to the written Kashmīrī Śaiva tradition, she has no way to share her experiences with those who understand her. She also does not have recourse to the experiences of women, oral or written, that preceded her. In contrast to Lallā, the seventeenth century Kashmīrī mystic poet Rūpa Bhavānī specifically mentions the sustenance she derives from Lallā's life and her verses. Even though Rūpa finds Lallā's life continuing into her own, she does not feel the need to become a wandering ascetic. In spite of leaving home for brief periods of time, Rūpa nonetheless remains integrally connected to her family and community.

As Lallā begins her quest, she describes worldly life in terms of a river, which she needs to cross in order to reach the other shore. Her body is a "boat" adrift in the material world that is

---

[2] Śiva represents the male principle and Śakti the female principle. Śakti is active and in this creative role, she is identified with nature, whereas Śiva is identified with pure spirit.

a temporary residence now. She has yet to prepare herself physically and mentally for the journey. In order to steer the "body-boat" to reach the other shore where her real home lies, she must train her mind in sustained and focused attention:

> My path to this world was direct,
> the road back is not.
> The day passed by the riverside—
> not a penny is in my pocket.
> What would I pay to be ferried across? (V 1)

Lallā compares her weak will at this early stage of her quest to an "untwisted rope" which is not strong enough to pull the "boat" she is riding. It is like a "grass arrow fitted on a wooden bow." Her novice self is like "a shop without a lock in the midst of the marketplace" and as such an easy target for worldly desires that can rob her of her aspiration to move forward on her path:

> A grass arrow fitted on a wooden bow I am.
> My palace is in the hands of an ignorant carpenter.
> In the midst of the market place I am
> like a shop without a lock.
> My body has become bereft of sanctity.
> Who would understand my plight? (V 7)

In this unexplored territory, Lallā's journey is perilous. She is overwhelmed as she finds herself alone without any family or community support. She describes her body as a "cauldron" full of sensory impressions that tie her to the world. In yet another verse, she compares her body to a house and her sense organs to its doors and windows that must be kept shut in order for her to stay focused on her practice. Her scattered attention is like the "water oozing from unbaked clay saucers" and her restless mind is like a horse galloping away from one thought to another. The "mind-horse" needs to be brought under control in order to experience her higher Self.

> The mind-horse wanders all over
> with the flicker of an eyelid,

traveling a hundred thousand leagues.
Whoever holds the reins
with self-restraint and discrimination
succeeds in controlling
the inhaled and the exhaled breath. (V 59)

In a world bustling with activity all around her, Lallā strives
to be detached. However, detachment is difficult to achieve.
She uses the image of sugar candy to personify all enjoyable
desires that pull her toward the world of sensory pleasures.

Loosened is the shoulder knot
of my bundle of candy.
Bent like a bow is my body.
How can I carry this burden?
My guru's words
to achieve detachment are painful.
A flock without a shepherd I am—
how can I carry this burden? (V 6)

As she continues on her path, she exercises rigorous self-
discipline. The following verse poignantly reflects her effort
to tear herself away from the comforts and pleasures of life
by reminding herself of their transitory nature:

I gently lament for you.
Mind, you are in love with illusion.
Not a shadow of this worldly splendor
will accompany you.
Oh, why do you forget your real nature? (V 5)

The path that she has chosen for herself is not easy to
follow. She has yet to reach the level of detachment that
would help her overcome the desire to live a worldly life.

Lallā's intuition is forged in the furnace of suffering. She
endures ill treatment at home. But her walking out also gives
her strength. Estrangement from society becomes her shield
in the early stages of her quest. Her refusal to conform to
social conventions is not taken kindly by community
members who gossip about her and find her lifestyle
scandalous.

As a wandering ascetic, insults and abuses come her way. She sometimes succeeds in keeping her spirits high, while at other times she is filled with self-pity. In order to make progress in her practice and reach her desired goal, Lallā feels the need to leave all negative emotions behind. Thus, she says:

> The chain of embarrassment will break
> when I can tolerate taunts
> and mocking words.
> The robe of self-pity will burn away
> when the inner unbridled horse is under control. (V 8)

A story about her relates how street urchins used to hurl insults at her. A kind-hearted shopkeeper, a cloth merchant, witnessing this scene, scolds the youngsters and sends them away. Lallā calmly asks the shopkeeper to give her a long piece of cloth. When he complies, she tells him to cut it into two equal parts and weigh them separately. She then drapes one piece on her left shoulder and the second on her right shoulder and goes away. As soon as someone calls her a bad name, she ties a knot in the piece on her right shoulder and as she is shown respect by somebody else, she ties a knot in the other piece on her left shoulder. In the evening she brings back the two pieces of cloth to the shopkeeper and asks him to weigh them once again—both pieces weigh exactly as they had before. The number of knots signifying good or bad words has had no effect on the weight of each half of the piece of cloth. She thus conveys to the shopkeeper her equanimity in the face of respect or ridicule shown by others towards her:

> Even if thousands of abuses
> are hurled at me,
> I am not hurt in my heart.
> If I am a devotee
> of all-pervading Self—Śaṅkara,
> ashes will not soil the mirror. (V 11)

Lallā's verses usually lack the devotional fervor of Bhakti poets. like Mīrābai. Hence, it is easy to overlook the significance of "love" in her oeuvre. A few of her verses, however, do refer to the world of emotions. Intense yearning and love, she realizes, is the first step to get closer to the object of her quest. As a devotee of Śiva, she "suffers the fire of love" as she awakens Śiva within her. She conveys the experience of "awakening her darling" by using vivid images of "grinding" the heart in the "mortar of love," and "burning" and "roasting" it and "tasting" it herself.

> I ground my heart in the mortar of love.
> Evil thoughts left me
> and I became calm.
> I burned and roasted it
> and tasted it myself.
> How do I know
> if this practice will let me live or die? (V 18)

The love experienced with so much intensity is not the egoistical or narcissistic love, but rather love for the boundless reality within her. This is a love in which fulfillment is not a let-down, a love that remains forever fresh. The inner-directed love for Śiva thus constitutes the first step in the unfolding of her spiritual journey.

> Awakening in the early dawn,
> I summoned the restless mind.
> Enduring the pain,
> I devoted myself to god.
> Saying "I am Lallā, I am Lallā,"
> I awakened my darling.
> On becoming one with him,
> I purified my mind and body. (V 19)

In the fire of this love, Lallā forges her mind and body. She has momentary glimpses of the bliss of communion with Śiva which prepare her for more advanced stages of her practice.

Lallā's life can be compared to that of the medieval Śaiva mystic poet Akkā Mahādevī who lived in South India in the 12th century. Mahādevī belonged to the Vīraśaiva religious reform movement of mystics who rejected caste and class hierarchy and protested against ritualistic and orthodox Śaiva religion focused around complex daily rituals. She is known to have defied social rules and customs, thrown away modesty and wandered in a nude state, her body covered with her long hair. Mahādevī's poetry (*vācanas*), spoken in Kannada, shows a curious blend of bhakti tradition and Śaiva monotheism. In these, she expresses her love and devotion to Cenna Mallikārjuna, a form of Śiva. Describing him as her husband, lover, and father, her only aspiration is to be united with him.

Mahādevī uses the genre of love poetry to articulate her spiritual experience. When she visits the school of Vīraśaiva mystics, founded by Basavanna in Kalyana, she engages in a verbal exchange with the head of the assembly, Allama Prabhu, who tests her to see if she is worthy to join the fellowship. The first question he asks her is to identify her husband if she wants to stay. Mahādevī replies that she is married to Cenna Mallikārjuna. The verbal exchange that ensues soon after shows the assembly her advanced spiritual state and she is welcomed with open arms. In some of her poems, she describes her initiation into the fellowship in terms of a marriage ritual when she becomes Cenna Mallikārjuna's wife:

> Setting a canopy of fire
> Over an altar made of water,
> Spreading a hailstone carpet,
> He came and wedded
> A headless bridegroom to a legless bride.
> They gave me to a life never to be shaken off!
> They married me to a groom
> Named Cenna Mallikārjuna[3]

---

[3] Akka Mahādevī, quoted in Swamy's *The Vīraśaiva Saints*, p. 104.

Mahādevī's poetry is similar to Mīrā in its bhakti
orientation, even as it is closer to Lallā's in its philosophic
and esoteric content. Unlike Lallā, however, Mahādevī makes
an aesthetic dimension central to her spiritual quest. In all
her poems the signature line refers to Cenna Mallikārjuna,
(translated both as "lovely Arjuna, Lord of goddess Mallika"
or "lovely lord, white as jasmine"). The latter suggests both
the aroma as well as the beauty of jasmine flowers. The
qualifier "white" represents her quest to be united with a
state that is devoid of all distinctions. While Mahādevī makes
human love a metaphor for mystic experience, Lallā makes
the image of ascetic Śiva her ideal. One could perhaps say
that what Mahādevī acquired through intense *bhaktiyoga*
(path of devotion), Lallā achieved through concentrated
jñānayoga (path of knowledge). The poetry of both women
reveals their knowledge of the esoteric aspects of Śaivism.
The paths they adopted were different, even as it seems their
final objective was the same.

Exploring the Inner Landscape

A mystic's journey involves the exploration of the inner
landscape of mind. Intially the world appears fragmented
and divided, populated with a variety of colors, shapes and
forms. The mystic's intuition reveals that permeating all the
variety and diversity is the colorless, shapeless and formless
light of consciousness.

Many of Lallā's verses specifically refer to Śaiva practices
centered on breathing to reach inner focus, which is
necessary to have higher states of awareness.

> Slowly through practicing breath control,
> the lamp shone
> and I saw my true nature.
> The inner light I realized—
> caught it in darkness and seized it. (V 46)

Her 'true nature' is the realization of the unity of the Self and the self or, in other words, the non-dual nature of reality. It is essential to let go of ego-consciousness in order to have such an experience. Since self-consciousness always keeps dividing and separating what is otherwise continuous and interpenetrating the conflict from duality persists. In order to clarify the relationship of the Self to the self, Lallā uses the metaphor of water and two other of its forms as they appear in nature: ice and snow. When the clouds disperse and the sun reveals its face, both ice and snow melt and turn into water, even though as ice and snow they have their own unique properties as well as modes of existence specific to their condition:

> Cold changes water into ice or snow.
> Discernment shows the three different states
> are not really different.
> When the sun of consciousness shines,
> the plurality is dissolved into oneness.
> The universe appears throughout permeated with Śiva.
> (V 63)

The shining of the sun of consciousness here refers to the realization of one's unity with the Self when the subject/object duality is erased and the Self, the quintessential nature of both, is revealed in its fullness.

To elaborate further on this relationship, she compares the Self to the axle of a grindstone. The axle must be set into motion for the wheat to move into the middle portion to be ground between the flat stones of the grindstone. Without this action, the movement of the grindstone and consequently, that of the wheat would come to a standstill. The moving axle is the driving force that brings about the motion of the flat stones, which pulls the wheat in to be ground into fine flour:

> The grindstone moves
> when set in motion.
> The axle knows the mystery
> of the grindstone.
> When the grindstone moves,

> fine flour comes out
> as the wheat moves by itself
> into the grindstone
> to be crushed. (V 103)

The grindstone thus becomes a metaphor for human existence. To live an enlightened life, the self-aware individual takes control of the axle of life, the higher Self, in order to experience fully the dynamic weaving of the world from the light of consciousness.

Most of Lallā's verses thus comment on the continuity between the self and the Self and between the Self and the world. Individuals are not islands in the ocean of consciousness, but rather waves in the ocean, as their existence is intricately bound up with the reality out of which they emerge. She captures this continuity in the image of the Self as a net spread over the entire phenomenal world, in the meshes of which the individual existence takes shape.

> Śiva is like a fine net spread everywhere,
> subtly permeating the physical world.
> If you don't see him while alive,
> how can you do so when dead?
> Through self-introspection,
> remove the self from within yourself. (V 145)

Lallā relies on metaphors and similes from day to day life to convey her experiences, as she tailors her message to the audience she is addressing. She sometimes speaks of her experience in terms of devotion to Śiva, while at other times she describes Śiva as the transcendental reality. Elsewhere, she speaks of the need to do away entirely with duality of all kinds in order to find a new space for the actualizing self outside any dualistic framework. The most profound of Lallā's verses, then, convey the experience that is beyond any anthropomorphic representation. She compares the advanced stages of her spiritual journey to traveling through a field of void and her ultimate goal is to realize the state of *śūnya* or nothingness.

Teachings

Even though leading the life of an ascetic, Lallā is very much concerned with the welfare of the people in her community. Śaiva teachings were traditionally imparted only to a select few during her time. Lallā is the first woman we know of who openly speaks of these practices to common people in vernacular Kashmīrī language.

Lallā criticizes the elite who take great pride in their scholarly achievements. The scholar's knowledge of the tradition, she says, is no guarantee of genuine insight or wisdom. This view reflects her own position in relation to the Śaiva tradition in that she leaves the written tradition behind, and focuses on direct experience of that which is the subject of elaboration and discussion in the written tradition. In one of her verses she says that she learned some things from books, but others she learned through direct experience. Thus, she emphasizes direct experience above any elaborate study of religious texts. The strongest current that runs through Lallā's verses reflects her belief that enlightened perspective can be realized through one's own striving.

Lallā was quite secular in her outlook, which is perhaps the reason why both Hindus and Muslims have held her in such high esteem. She preached tolerance towards religious practices other than one's own and she refrained from identifying herself with any sect or religion. Legends speak of the Sūfī and Hindu mystics gathering together frequently to exchange ideas and experiences. The Sūfī mystics lived simple and devout lives and never abdicated their missionary spirit. Lallā's emphasis on religious tolerance may have been influenced by this free association with Sūfī mystics of her time. Her belief in religious tolerance, however, is also in agreement with the monist Śaiva philosophy that is secular in its orientation.

In her verses Lallā critiques prescriptive religious practices of all kinds and advises people not to differentiate between Hindus and Muslims, as Śiva, which is their own Self, is omniscient and hence, beyond sectarian divisions. People might call this state Śiva, Keśava, Mahāvira, or Buddha, but these are just different names assigned to the same reality:

> The Self may be named Śiva,
> Keśava, or Mahāvīra
> or the lotus born Buddha.
> Whatever name it may have, .
> may it set free a weakling like me
> from worldly afflictions. (V 12)

As a critic of prescriptive religious practices, Lallā points to the limited use of external worship or rituals of various kinds. Objects of ritual worship, for example, kuś grass, sesame seeds, lamp or water, are unnecessary in the same way as is making offerings of animals to idols. Thus, reciting prayers, chanting mantras, or turning rosary beads are not enough to move forward and make progress in spiritual awareness. Parrots can be taught to recite the name of Rāma, so repetition of a mantra in itself does not lead to self - knowledge:

> Those without discernment, dear,
> read religious books
> as parrots recite "Rāma" in a cage.
> Reading the Gītā becomes an excuse—
> I have read the Gītā
> and I am still reading it. (V 117)

She urges people not to confuse the aids to focus attention, for example, rituals or chanting of mantras, with the ultimate goal of the spiritual journey, which is self realization. Religious scriptures, according to her, are beneficial for beginners, but those who make a religion of recitation of scriptures are chasing illusion. The genuine progress in the spiritual journey of the novice happens only when the mind and the heart work together. Through various breathing exercises as well as meditations, the novice undergoes a transformation of mind and body and achieves higher levels of awareness.

Lallā regards people who are consumed by their quest for deeper answers as fully awake and those immersed only in material reality as asleep. The real temple is within each individual. Thus, she says, self-knowledge cannot be acquired by merely going to temples or going on pilgrimages:

> Some renounce their home,
> and some their hermitage.
> All is futile
> if the mind is not under control.
> Meditate on your breath
> day and night,
> and stay wherever you are. (V 98)

To those desiring to live enlightened lives, Lallā advises moderation in drinking, eating, and clothing. She does not approve of starving the body through fasting or religious austerities. The real religious practice is to engage in actions performed in the spirit of detachment.

> Don't torture your body
> with thirst and starvation.
> When the body is exhausted,
> take care of it.
> Cursed be your fasts
> and religious ceremonies.
> Be good to others—
> that is the real religious practice. (V 118)

According to a legend, once her teacher Śrīkaṇtha was bathing in the river, while Lallā was cleaning the outside of a pot full of dirt a little upstream. Śrīkaṇtha, puzzled, asks her how she could possibly have a clean pot if she scrubbed it only from the outside. Lallā responds that how could he cleanse his body through bathing alone, without purifying his thoughts and feelings. This legend could be understood as Lallā's critique of hypocritical practices of people who engaged in ritual purification, while in the secular world they performed acts oppressive to others. Habitually performing religious practices, she says, might give people satisfaction in engaging in something spiritual but in reality would do nothing to expand the limited vision that leads to religious bigotry and non-tolerance. She compares the path of wisdom to a kitchen garden that needs to be nurtured with self-restraint where good actions are performed with detachment.

Lallā is one of the few medieval women mystic poets worldwide who have left behind a legacy of great relevance to contemporary society. She urges people to have courage to seek their inner vision, instead of leading a life governed merely by social expectations. She brings our attention to the need for a morality based on honesty and personal responsibility, and provokes us to look beyond the veil of prohibitions and constraints imposed by social and religious institutions. The oral transmission of her verses over centuries testifies to her perennial appeal to people of all faiths.

Lallā lived during a time of great change and her words were meant to be a vehicle for change. Her verses can be seen as an instrument of change—an inner change—that must go hand in hand with any external political change of society. She urges us to create a society based on equality, mutual respect, and caring. Since the contemporary era also constitutes an age of transition, though now on a global scale, the themes that permeate her verses are as valid today as they were in medieval Kashmīr. For that reason, Lallā's verses are as relevant today as they were more than six centuries ago. No sanctified place or relic exists from Lallā's time marking the place of her death. A legend says when she died a bright flame shot forth from her body and vanished from sight. The flame might have vanished, but it continues to inform the spirit of Lallā's verses which enlighten and amaze us even today.

Key to Pronounciation

Key to Pronounciation of Kaśmīrī Verses Written in Modified Devanāgarī Script

A. Vowels

1. अ or (')	as in	अंड	=	half
		अंछ	=	eye
2. आ or (ो)	as in	दांर	=	window
		लांर	=	cucumber
3. उ or ()	as in	तुर	=	tatter
		खुर	=	slip
4. इ or (॒)	as in	त॒र	=	cold
		द्रफ	=	incense
5. ओ॒ or (॒)	as in	ओ॒न	=	blind
		सो॒न	=	deep

B. Consonants

1. च	c	as in	चोन	=	your
2. च़	ts	as in	च़ास	=	cough
			च़ल	=	go away
3. छ़	tsh	as in	छ़ाय	=	shadow
			गछ़	=	go
4. ज	z	as in	जल	=	water
			जाल	=	net

Sounds in Kaśmīrī and the Diacritical Marks used in the Romanized Script

t = त   th = थ   ṭ = ट   ṭh = ठ
d = द   ḍ = ड

ŏ = short sound of o as in Kashmīrī क्वछ़ kŏcha = lap; mŏkh = face
ĕ = short sound of e as in Kashmīrī स्यख sĕkh = sand; च्यथ tsĕth = mind

Lallā's Verses

The River of Life

1

आयस वते गंयस नु वते
सुमन स्वथि मंज़ लूस्तुम दोह
चंदस वुछुम तु हार नु अते
नाव् तारस दिम् क्याह बोह

āyas vate gayas na vate
suman svathimaṅz lūstum doh
caṅdas vuchum ta hār na ate
nāva tāras dima kyāh bŏh

My path to this world was direct,
the road back is not.
The day passed by the riverside—
not a penny is in my pocket.
What would I pay to be ferried across?

2

आमि पन॒ संद॒रस नावि छस लमान
कति बोज़ि दय म्योन म्यॊति दियि तार
आम्यन टाक्यन पोज़ ज़न शमान
जुव छुम ब्रमान गर॒ गछह॒

āmi pana sadaras nāvi chas lamān
kati bozi day myon mĕti diyi tār
āmĕn tākĕn poñ zan shamān
zuv chum bramān gara gatshaha

I pull the boat with an untwisted rope.
Will god hear me
and help me across?
Water oozes from unbaked clay saucers.
My heart desires to go home.

3

हा च्यत्ता कव छुय लोगमुत परमस
कव गोय अपज़िस पज़युक ब्रोंत
दोशिबोज़ वश कोरनख परदरमस
यिन गछन ज्यन मरनस क्रोंत

hā tsĕtta kava chuy lŏgmut paramas
kava gŏy apazis pazyuk bront
dŏśibŏz vash kŏrnakh pardarmas
yina gatshana zĕna maranas kront

Hey mind, why are you attached
to the external world?
Why do you mistake
illusory for the real?
Lack of wisdom has won you over
to the wrong path—
resigned to coming and going,
death and rebirth.

4

आयस कमि दिशि त॒ कमि वते
गछ॒ कमि दिशि कव॒ जान॒ वथ
अन्ति दाय लगिमय तते
छांनिस फो॒कस कांह ति नो सथ

āyas kami dishi ta kami vate
gatsha kami dishi kava zāna vath
anti dāy lagimay tate
chănis phŏkas kănh ti no sath

From which direction did I come
and what road did I take?
Which direction shall I go?
How will I know the path?
Right guidance will finally come to my aid—
empty breath has no value.

5

लॅलिथ लॅलिथ वदय बो॒ह वाय
च्यत्ता मुहुच प्यॅयिय माय
रोज़िय नो पत॒ लोह लङ्ग॒र॒च छा॒य
निज़॒ स्वरूप क्याह मो॒ठुय हाय

lalith lalith vaday bŏh vāy
tsĕtta muhuc pĕyiy māy
roziy no pata loha langarac ṭshāy
niz svarūp kyāh mŏṭhuy hāy

I gently lament for you.
Mind, you are in love with illusion.
Not a shadow of this worldly splendor
will accompany you.
Oh, why do you forget your real nature?

6

नाबद्य बारस अटगंड ड्योल गोम
दिह कान होल गोम ह्रक् क्यहो
ग्वर सुन्द वनुन रावन त्योल प्योम
पहलि रोस्त ख्योल गोम ह्रक् क्यहो

nābadi bāras aṭagaṇḍ ḍyŏl gom
diha-kān hŏl gom hyaka kyaho
gvara sund vanun rāvan tyŏl pyom
pahali-rŏst khyŏl gom hyaka kyaho

Loosened is the shoulder knot
of my bundle of candy.
Bent like a bow is my body.
How can I carry this burden?
My guru's words
to achieve detachment are painful.
A flock without a shepherd I am—
how can I carry this burden?

7

हचिवि हॅरिंजि प्यंचिव कान गोम
अबख छान प्योम यथ राज़ुदाने
मंज़बाग बाज़रस कुल्फ़ रोस्त वान गोम
तिर्थ-रोस्त पान गोम कुस मालि ज़ाने

hacivi härinji pĕtsiv-kān gom
abakh chān pyom yath rāzdāne
manzbāg bāzaras kulfa-rŏst vān gom
tirtha-rŏst pān gom kus māli zāne

A grass arrow fitted on a wooden bow I am.
My palace is in the hands
of an ignorant carpenter.[1]
In the midst of the market place I am
like a shop without a lock.
My body has become bereft of sanctity.
Who would understand my plight?

---

[1] The "grass arrow," "ignorant carpenter," and "shop without a lock"
are metaphors for the novice self.

8

मंदुछि हाँकता कर छेनयम
यलि ह्यंडुन गेलुन असुन प्राव्
आरुक जाम् करसना दज़्यम
यलि अन्द्रयुम खारयुक रोज़्यम वार्

mandachi hänkal kar tshenĕm
yali hĕdun gelun asun prāva
āruk jāma karsanā dazĕm
yali andryum khāryuk rozĕm vāra

The chain of embarrassment will break
when I can tolerate taunts
and mocking words.
The robe of self-pity will burn away
when the inner unbridled horse[2] is under control.

---

[2] The "unbridled horse" represents the scattered nature of restless
mind skipping from thought to thought aimlessly.

9

रुत त् क्रुत सोरुय पज्यम
कनन न् बोजुन अंछयन न् बाव
ओरुक दपुन यलि वोन्दि वुज्यम
रंत्लदीप प्रज़ल्यम वरज़नि वाव्

rut ta krut soruy pazĕm
kanan na bozun achĕn na bāva
oruk dapun yĕli vŏndi vuzĕm
ratandīp prazalĕm varzani vāva

Both good and bad, I must endure.
My ears don't hear,
and my eyes don't see.
When the inner Self
awakens in my heart,
the lamp will shine
even in the midst of a tornado.

10

गाटुलाह अख वुछुम ब्वछि सा॑त्य मरान
पन ज॒न हरान पो॒हनि वावलाह
न्य॑षबो॒द अख वुछुम वाज़स मारान
तन॒ लल॒ बो॒ह प्रारान छ॒यन्यम न॒ प्राह

gātulāh akh vuchum bŏchi säty marān
pan zan harān pŏhani vāvalāh
nĕshabŏd akh vuchum vāzas mārān
tana lalla bŏh prārān tshĕnĕm na prāh

A wise one I saw dying of hunger
just as leaves fall
with the early winter wind.
And I saw a fool beating his cook.
Since then I, Lallā, am waiting
for the moment
when my worldly ties are severed.

11

आंसा बोल पंडिन्यम सासा
म्यं मनिवासा खीद न ह्यंये
बोह योद सहज़ शंकर बंखच़ आसां
मंकुरिस सासा मल क्याह प्यंये

äsā bol paḍinĕm sāsā
mĕ manivāsā khīd na hĕye
bŏh yŏd sahaza śaṅkara-bakts āsā
makaris sāsā mal kyāh pĕye

Even if thousands of abuses
are hurled at me,
I am not hurt in my heart.
If I am a devotee
of all-pervading Self— Śaṅkara[3],
ashes will not soil the mirror.

---

[3] Śaṅkara is a name for Śiva.

12

शिव वा कीशव वा जिन. वा
कम‌लज़ नाथ नाम दा॑रिन युह
म्यं अबलि का॑सितन बव‌रो‌ज़
सुह वा सुह वा सुह वा सुह

śiva vā kīśava vā jin vā
kamalaza nāth nāma därin yuh
mĕ abali käsitan bavarŏz
suh vā suh vā suh vā suh

The Self may be named Śiva,
Keśava, or Mahāvīra
or the lotus-born Buddha.
Whatever name it may have,
may it set free a weakling like me
from worldly afflictions.

Crossing the River

13

लल् बोह् द्रायस कपूसि पोशिचि सांचुई
कांडि त् दूनि कंरनम यचय लथ
तुयि यलि खांरिनम् ज्ञांविजि तंये
बोवरि वान गंयम अलांज़य लथ

lalla bŏh drāyas kapasi pośici sätsiy
kādi ta dūni karnam yatsay lath
tuyi yali khärinam zäviji taye
bovari vāna gayam alānzay lath

I, Lallā, set out hoping to bloom
like a cotton flower.
The ginner and the carder gave me hard blows.
After the spinner spun me into fine yarn,
I was stretched on the loom
in the weaver's shop.

14

दोॗब्य यलि छाँवनस दोॗब्य कनि प्यठ॒य
सज॒ त॒ साबन मछ॒नम यच॒य
साँचि॒ यलि फिरनम हनि हनि काँच॒इ
अद॒ ललि म्यं प्राँवम परम गथ

dŏbi yali chävanas dŏbi-kani pĕṭhay
saza ta sāban matshnam yatsay
sätsi yali phiranam hani hani kätsiy
ada lalli mĕ prävam parma gath

When the washerman dashed me
on a slab of stone,
rubbing me with much soap and washing soda
and the tailor cut me into bits with scissors,
I, Lallā, attained supreme bliss.

15

नाथा न॒ पान न॒ पर ज़ोनुम
सदै बूदुम यिकुय दिह
त्र॒ बोह बोह त्र॒ म्यूल न ज़ोनुम
त्र॒ कुस बोह क्वस॒ छु सन्दीह

nāthā na pān na par zonum
sadai būdum yekuy dih
tsa bŏh bŏh tsa myūl na zonum
tsa kus bŏh kŏsa chuh sandīh

Lord, the Self in myself and others
I did not recognize.
I have always known only this body.
You and I are joined in one,
I did not know.
My doubts remained:
who are you and who am I?

16

क्याह कर् पांच्न दह्न त् काहन
वोक्षुन यथ ल्य॒जि कॅरिथ यिम गंय
सॉरिय सम्हन यॅथ्य रज्जि लम्हन
अद् क्याज़ि राविहे काहन गाव

kyāh kara päntsan dahan ta kāhan
vŏkhshun yath lĕji karith yim gay
säriy samahan yĕthi razi lamahan
ada kyāzi rāvihe kāhan gāv

What will I do
with the five, the ten, and the eleven?
They have all emptied out the cauldron.
If all had come together
and pulled the rope,
the eleven would not have lost the cow.[4]

---

[4] The "cauldron" is the physical body, the "five" are five *bhūtas* or principles of experience, the "ten" are the five sense organs plus the five organs of action, and the "eleven" are these ten organs and the mind. The "cow" symbolilzes the Śiva consciousness.

17

यिमय श्यं ह्यं तिमय श्यं म्यं
श्यामगला ह्यं ब्योन तांठिस
युहोय ब्यंनबीद ह्यं त म्यं
ह्रं श्यंन स्वामी बोह श्यंयि मशिस

yimay śĕ tsĕ timay śĕ mĕ
śyāmagalā tsĕ byŏn tä̃this
yuhŏy bĕnabīd tsĕ ta mĕ
tsa śĕn svāmī bŏh śĕyi maśis

You have the same six attributes[5] as I do.
Blue-throated One,[6]
without you I am afflicted.
The difference between you and me—
you are master of the six,
whereas I am deluded by the six.

---

[5] The six attributes are anger, bewilderment, arrogance, passion, jealousy, and avarice.

[6] Śiva is also called the "Blue-throated One" in the mythological literature.

18

लोलकि वोखल वलिंज पिशिम
क्वकल त्रजिम त् रूज्रस रस्
बुजुम त् ज्रंजिम पानस चशिम
कव् ज्ञान तव् सांत्य मर् किन् लस्

lolaki vŏkhala väliṅj piśim
kvakal tsajim ta rūzas rasa
buzam ta zäjim pānas caśim
kava zāna tava sätya mara kina lasa

I ground my heart in the mortar of love.
Evil thoughts left me
and I became calm.
I burned and roasted it
and tasted it myself.
How do I know
if this practice will let me live or die?

19

पोत जूनि वंथिथ मोत बोलनोवुम
दग ललनांवुम दयि संज़ि प्रहे
ललि ललि करान लाल वुज़नोवुम
मीलिथ तस मन श्रोच्योम दहे

pŏt zūni vathith mŏt bolanovum
dag lalanävam dayi sanzi prahe
lalli lalli karān lāla vuzanovum
mīlith tas man shrotsyom dahe

Awakening in the early dawn,
I summoned the restless mind.
Enduring the pain,
I devoted myself to god.
Saying "I am Lallā, I am Lallā,"
I awakened my darling.
On becoming one with him,
I purified my mind and body.

20

ल्यक् त् थवक् प्यठ शेरि ह्यच्म्
न्यन्दा सपनिम पथ ब्रोंठ तान्य
लल छयस कल ज़ांह नो छयनिम
अद यलि सपनिस व्यपिहे क्याह

lĕka ta thŏka pĕth sheri hĕtsam
nyandā sapanim path bronṭh tāni
lalla chĕs kal zānh no tshĕnim
ada yali sapanis vĕpihe kyāh

I endured verbal abuse and slander.
Scandals broke out
about my past and present.
I am Lallā
and my yearning never stopped.
When I achieved my goal,
nothing affected me.

21

ज़नम प्रॉविथ व्यबव न॒ छोंडुम
लूबन बूगन ब॑र॒म न॒ प्रय
सो॒मुय आहार स्यठाह ज़ोनुम
च्योलुम द्व:ख॒ वाव पोलुम दय

zanam prävith vĕbav na tshoṇḍum
lūban būgan baram na pray
sŏmuy āhār sĕṭhāh zonum
tsolum dŏkh-vāv polum day

In life I did not desire affluence.
Nor did I love greed or enjoyment of luxuries.
Moderate meals I considered sufficient for me.
I endured suffering and poverty
and remained devoted to god.

22

ग्वरस पृछ्योम सासि लटे
यस न॒ कॅह वनान तस क्याह नाव
पृछान पृछान थचिस त॒ लूसस
कॅहनस निशि क्याहताम द्राव

gvaras pritshom sāsi late
yas na kĕnh vanān tas kyāh nāv
pritshān pritshān thacis ta lūsas
kĕnhnasa nishi kyāhtām drāv

Again and again I asked my guru—
What is the name of the undefinable?
Repeated questioning
tired and exhausted me—
something has come out of this nothing.

23

लल॒ ब॒ोह लूसंस छांडान त॒ गारान
हल म्यं क॒ोरमस रसनिशांतिय
वुछुन ह्यॊतमस तांर्य डीठिमस बरन
म्यति कल गनेयम त॒ ज़ोगमस ततिय

lalla bŏh lūsas tshāṇḍān ta gārān
hal mĕ kŏrmas rasaniśatiy
vuchun hyŏtmas tärya dīṭhimas baran
mĕti kal gañeyam ta zogmas tatiy

I, Lallā, became tired
searching so eagerly.
I put more effort into it
than I was capable of.
When I started seeing,
I saw the doors bolted—
my yearning increased
and I kept a watch there.

24

अंद्रिय आयस त्रंद॑रय गारान
गारान आयस हिह्न हिह
त्रां॑य है नारान त्रां॑य है नारान
त्रां॑य है नारान यिम कम विह

andriy āyas tsandaray gārān
gārān āyas hihĕn hih
tsäy hai nārān tsäy hai nārān
tsäy hai nārān yim kam vih

From within I came searching for the moon.
I continued seeking similar symbols.
You are god[7],
you are god,
and you are god—
why these distinctions?

---

[7] The word "nārān" specifically means God Viṣṇu but also refers to any
god.

The Field of Void

25

ये ग्वरा परमीश्वरा
बावतम च्यं॒ छुय अन्तर व्यो॒द
द्रशिवय वो॒पदान कंद॒-पुरा
हुह कव॒ तूरुन त॒ हाह कव॒ तो॒त

ye gvarā paramīśvarā
bāvtam tsĕy chuy antar vyŏd
dvaśivay vŏpadān kanda-purā
huh kava türun ta hāh kava tŏt

You, guru, Parameśvara,
reveal to me the inner truth you know.
Both prāṇas arise
from the abode of the navel cakra.
Why is *huh* cold
and *hāh* hot?[8]

---

[8] In this and the next verse, Lallā refers to the meditation on the
inhaled and the exhaled breath, a basic practice of Kashmīrī Śaivism.
The *brahmarandhra* is the seventh cakra.

26

नाबिस्थानस छय प्रक्रथ जल॒व॒नी
हिदिस्ताम यंति प्राण वत॒गो॒त
ब्रह्माण्डस प्यठ सांत नद वहवनी
हुह तव॒ तुरुण त॒ हाह तव॒ तो॒त

nābisthānas chay prakrath zalavanī
hidistām yĕti prān vatagŏt
brahmāṇḍas pyetha sät nad vahavani
huh tava türun ta hāh tava tŏt

The region of the navel is naturally ablaze.
The breath moves up the throat
to the *brahmarandhra*
from which the river flows.
For this reason, *Huh* is cold
and *Hāh* is hot.

27

दिहचि लरि दारि-बर त्रोपरिम
प्राण-चूर रोटुम त द्युतमस दम
ह्रदयिचि कूठरि अन्दर गों्डुम
ओंमुकि चोबुक़ तुलिमस बम

dihaci lari dāri bar trŏparim
prāna tsūr rŏṭum ta dyutmas dam
hrĕdyici kūṭhari andar gŏṇdum
oṃaki cobuka tulimas bam

Doors and windows of my body I closed.
The prāṇa-thief I caught
and brought under control.
I tied it inside the chamber of my heart.
I whipped it with the syllable Oṃ.

28

ओंकार यलि लयि ओ्नुम
वुहि को्रुम फ्नुन पान
श्य वो्त त्राविथ त् सथ मार्ग रो्टुम
त्यलि ललـ बो्ह वा्चस प्रकाशस्थान

oṃkār yĕli layi ŏnum
vuhi kŏrum panun pān
śĕ vŏta trävith ta sath mārg rŏṭum
tĕli lalla bŏh vätsas prakāśasthān

I became absorbed in the sacred syllable Oṃ.
I burned myself like coal.
Leaving behind six paths,
I seized the seventh—
and then, I, Lallā, reached the abode of light.

29

च्यंत तुर्ग वगिह्वथ रोटुम
च्यलिथ मिलुविथ दशिनाडि वाव
तवय शशिकल व्यंगलिथ वछंम
शून्यस शून्याह मीलिथ गव

tsĕta turg vagihĕth rŏṭum
tsĕlith milavith dashināḍi vāv
tavay śaśikal vĕgalith vatshäm
śūnyas śūnyāh mīlith gav

I took the reins of the mind-horse.
Through practice, I learned breath control.
Then only the orb of the moon melted[9]
and dripped down into my body—
nothingness merged with nothingness.

---

[9] The "orb of the moon" refers to the seventh cakra.

30

अन्दर आसिथ न्यबर छोन्डुम
पवनन रगन कुरनम सथ
द्यान् किनि दय ज़ागि कीवल ज़ोनुम
रंग गव संगस मीलिथ क्यथ

andar äsith nĕbar tshonḍum
pavanan ragan karnam sath
dyāna kini day zagi kīval zonum
raṅg gav sangas mīlith kĕth

Though within, I searched outside.
The control of breath
soothed my inner channels.
Through meditation, I realized that
god and the world are one—
the manifest world merged with the unmanifest.

31

बान गोल तय प्रकाश आव जूने
ञ्रंदर गोल तय मोतुय च्यथ
च्यथ गोल तय केंहति ना कुने
गै भूर भुवाह स्वर व्यसर्जिथ क्यथ

bān gŏl tay prakāśa āv zūne
tsandar gŏl tay mŏtuy tsĕth
tsĕth gŏl tay keṅhti nā kune
gay bhūr bhuvāh svar vĕsarzith kĕth

The sun sets,
the moon shines.
The moon vanishes,
consciousness remains.
Consciousness disappears,
nothingness remains—
the physical, spiritual, and metaphysical
merge into nothingness.

32

पानस लागिथ रूदुख म्यं न्
म्यं च्यं छान्डान लूस्तुम दोह
पानस मंज़ यॆलि ड्यूठुख म्यं न्
म्यं च्यं त् पानस द्युतुम छोह

pānas lägith rūdukh mĕ tsa
mĕ tsĕ tshāṇḍān lūstum doh
pānas manz yĕli ḍyūṭhukh mĕ tsa
mĕ tsĕ ta pānas dyutum tshoh

When I was attached to the self,
you remained hidden from me.
Time passed as I searched for you.
When I saw you within—
you and I were united
in ecstasy.

33

दिशि आयस दश दिशि तीलिथ
च्यलिथ ऋोटुम शून्य अद् वाव
शिवय ड्यूठुम शायि शायि मीलिथ
श्यं त् त्रंह त्रांपिमस त् शिवय द्राव

dishi āyas dasha dishi tīlith
tsĕlith tsŏṭum śūnya ada vāv
śivay ḍyūṭhum śāyi śāyi mīlith
śĕ ta trĕh träpimas ta śivay drāv

After wandering in ten directions,
I found the true path.
Through breath control,
 I penetrated the void—
Śiva I saw permeating all.
Shutting the six and the three,[10]
I found Śiva the root cause of all.

---

[10] The "six" refers to the five sense organs and the mind, while the
"three" are the three body openings.

34

तन॒ मन॒ गयस बो॒ह तस कु॑नय
बूज़म सत॒च गन्टा वज़ान
तथ जायि दारनायि दारन रट॑म
अकाश त॒ प्रकाश को॒रुम सर॒

tana mana gayas bŏh tas kunay
buzam sataca gaṇṭā vazān
tath jāyi dārnāyi dāran raṭam
akāśa ta prakāśa kŏrum sara

Physically and mentally
absorbed in That,
I heard the bell of truth ring.
In that state, I meditated—
I realized the manifest
and the unmanifest.

A Lotus Blooms

35

शून्युक मांदान कोडुम पानस
म्यं ललि रूज़म न ब्वद न होश
बेदीय सपूनिस पानय पानस
अद् कमि गिलि फोल ललि पम्पोश

śūnyuk mädān koḍum pānas
mĕ lalli rūzam na bŏd na hosh
bedīy sapanis pānay pānas
ada kami gili phŏl lalli pamposh

Traversing the field of void alone,
I, Lallā, lost consciousness of myself.
On finding the secret of my Self,
a lotus bloomed in the mud for Lallā.[11]

---

[11] In Indian literature, the lotus is used to symbolize the higher self
that emerges out of the entangled world of senses.

36

गगन त्रांय बूतल त्रांय
त्रांय छुख द्यन पवन त् राथ
अर्ग च्न्दन पोश पोञ त्रांय
त्रांय छुख सोरुय त् लांगिज़िय क्याह

gagan tsäy būtal tsäy
tsäy chukh dĕn pavan ta rāth
arg tsandan poś poñ tsäy
tsäy chukh soruy ta lägiziy kyāh

You are the sky,
and you are the earth.
You are the day,
the night and the wind.
You are grain,
sandalwood, flowers, and water.
You are everything—
what should I offer you?

37

लतन हुन्द माज़ लार्योम वतन
अकिय हांवनम अकिचिय वथ
यिम यिम बोज़न तिम कोन् मतन
ललि बूज़ शतन कुनिय कथ

latan hund māz lāryom vatan
akiy hävnam akiciy vath
yim yim bozan tim kona matan
lalli būz shatan kuniy kath

Soles of my feet wore off
on different paths.
Only one showed me the true path.
Those who hear this,
why aren't they enamored?
Lallā heard but one word
in a hundred words.

38

पॅरुम पोलुम अपोॄरुय पुरुम
केसर् वन् वोलुम र्ंटिथ शाल
परस प्रोॄनुम त् पानस पोलुम
अद् गोम मोलूम त् ज़ीनिम हाल

parum polum apŏruy purum
kesara vana volum raṭith śāl
paras prŏnum ta pānas polum
ada gom molūm ta zīnim hāl

What I read, I followed.
The unreadable I realized
through direct experience.
I tamed the lion[12] from the forest like a jackal.
My teachings for others, I followed myself.
Then I attained knowledge
and achieved my goal.

---

[12] The lion is a metaphor for desires that continually entangle humans in worldly affairs. The subduing of desires is represented by the transformation of the lion into the jackal.

39

च्यथ नो॒वुय ऩंद्रम नो॒वुय
ज़लमय इ्यूठुम नवम नो॒वुय
यऩ प्यठ॒ ललि म्यं तन-मन नां॑वुय
तऩ लल॒ बो॒ह नवम नं॑वय छयस

tsĕth nŏvuy tsandaram nŏvuy
zalamay ḍyūṭhum navam nŏvuy
yana pĕtha lalli mĕ tan man nävuy
tana lalla bŏh navam navay chĕs

The consciousness is new,
and the moon is new.
I saw the whole universe
moment by moment renewed.
Ever since I, Lallā, cleansed
my body and mind,
I, Lallā, have become ever renewed.

40

दंमी डीठंम नद वहवनी
दंमी डयूठुम सुम नत् तार
दंमी डीठंम थंर् फव्लवनी
दंमी डयूठुम गुल नत् खार

damī ḍiṭham nad vahavanī
damī ḍyūṭhum sum nata tār
damī ḍiṭham thara phŏlavanī
damī ḍyūṭhum gul nata khār

Just now I saw a flowing river.
And then I saw a vast expanse of water
without a bridge or a ferry.
Just now I saw a shrub
with blooming flowers
and then I saw neither flowers nor thorns.[13]

---

[13] Lallā imagines herself outside time as she surveys the coming into existence and disappearance into nothingness of the objects and processes of the material world. The "flowing river," the "lake," the "shrub with blossoming flowers, the "fire ablaze in the hearth" all come and go.

41

ललॖ बोॖह द्रायस लोलॖ रे
छाँडान लूस्तुम द्यन क्योॖह राथ
वुछुम पंडिथ पनॢनि गरे
सुय म्यं रोॖटमस न्यछतुर तॖ साथ

lalla bŏh drāyas lola re
tshāṇḍān lūstum dyĕn kyŏh rāth
vuchum paṇḍith panani gare
suy mĕ rŏṭamas nĕchtur ta sāth

Full of love I set out.
Day and night I spent searching.
In my own home I met the Paṇḍit.
I caught him and this was
my auspicious moment.

42

परुन स्वलब पालुन द्वर्लब
सहज़ गारुन सिखिम त॒ क्रूठ
अब्यासु॒कि गनिरय शास्त्र मो॒ठुम
त्रीतन॒ आनन्द न्यश्चय गोम

parun svalab pālun dvarlab
sahaz gārun sikhim ta krūṭh
abyāsaki ganiray shāstra mŏṭhum
tsītan ānand nĕshcay gom

Easy to read, but hard to follow.
Attaining self-knowledge
is subtle and difficult.
Absorbed in practice,
I forgot the scriptures—
consciousness-bliss I realized.

43

यि यि करम को_रुम सुह अर्जुन
यि रसनि वो_न्त्रोरुम तिय मंथर
युहय लो_ग्मो दिहस पर्जुन
सुय यि परम शिवुन तंथर

yi yi karam kŏrum suh artsun
yi rasani vŏtsorum tiy manthr
yuhai lŏgamo dihas partsun
suy yi parama śivun tanthr

Deeds I performed became offerings.
Words I spoke became mantra.
Experiences my body had
were for self-knowledge.
This is the essence of Śiva's way.

44

मल वोन्दि ज़ोलुम
जिगर मोरुम
त्यंलि लल् नाव द्राम
यंलि दंलि त्रांविमस तती

mal vŏṅdi zolum
jigar morum
tĕli lalla nāv drām
yali dali trävimas tatī

Impurities of the heart I burned.
Desires I killed.
Lallā, my name, shone only
when I surrendered completely.

The Light of Consciousness

45

ह्नांय दीव् गर्तस त् दर्ती स्रज़ख
च्ये दीव दितिथ क्रन्ज़न प्रान
ह्नांय दीव् ठनि रोस्तुय वज़ख
कुस ज़ानि दीव् चोन परिमान

tsäy dīva gartas ta dartī srazakh
tsĕy dīva ditith kranzan prān
tsäy dīva ṭhani rŏstuy vazakh
kus zāni dīva con parimān

You, god, permeate the creation on the earth.
You, god, give life to matter.
You, god, resonate without sound.
Who can fathom you?

46

दमाह दम को_रमस दमनहाले
प्रज़ल्योम दीफ त_ ननेयम ज़ाथ
अन्द्रियुम प्रकाश न्यंबर छो_टुम
गटि रोटुम त_ क रमस थफ

damāh dam kŏrmas damanhāle
prazalyom dīph ta nañeyam zāth
andrium prakāśa nĕbar tshŏṭum
gaṭi roṭum ta karmas thaph

Slowly through practicing breath control,
the lamp shone
and I saw my true nature.
The inner light I realized—
caught it in darkness and seized it.

47

ग्यानुकि अम्बर पांरिथ तने
यिम पद ललि दपि तिम ह्यदि आंख
कारन् प्रनवकि लयि कोर लले
च्यथ-ज्योति कांसन मरनन्य शांख

gyanki ambar pärith tane
yim pad lalli dapi tim hrĕdi ankh
kārana pranavaki layi kŏr lalle
tsĕth-jyoti käsan maranañi shankh

Wear the garments of wisdom.
Inscribe verses recited by Lallā
in your heart.
Through *pranava*[14] Lallā was absorbed
in the light of consciousness.
She overcame the fear of death.

---

[14] *Pranava* involves meditation on the sacred syllable Oṃ.

48

च्यदानंदस ग्यान् प्रकाशस
यिमव च्यून तिम ज़ीवन्ती मोक्ष
व्यशमस सम्सारुनिस पाशयस
अबोध गंडाह शथ शथ दितिय

tsĕdānandas gyāna prakāśas
yimav tsyūn tim zīvantī mŏkht
vĕśamas samsāranis pāśyas
abŏdh gaṇḍah śath śath ditiy

Those who achieve light-consciousness-bliss
are liberated while alive.
Tangled in the net of worldly existence,
ignorant people tie a hundred knots.

49

परान परान ज्यव ताल फंजिम
च्यं युगि क्रिय तंजिम नु ज़ांह
सुमरन फिरान न्योठ तु आंगज़ गंजिम
मनुच् दुयि मालि त्रजिम नु ज़ांह

parān parān zyav tāl phajim
tsĕ yugi kriy tajim na zāṅh
sumran phirān nyoṭh ta ŏṅgaj gajim
manaca duyi māli tsajim na zāṅh

Reading and reciting continuously
turned my tongue and palate sore—
I never found a practice befitting you.
Turning the rosary beads
wore out my thumb and finger—
yet my mind's confusion, my dear,
did not leave me.

50

ग्वरन वो<u>न</u>नम कुनुय वच्चुन
न्यबर दो<u>प</u>नम अन्द्रय अच्चुन
सुय गव ललि म्यं वाख. त् वच्चुन
तवय म्यं ह्योतुम नंगय नच्चुन

gvaran vŏnanam kunuy vatsun
nĕbara dŏpanam andaray atsun
suy gav lalli mĕ vākh ta vatsun
tavay mĕ hyŏtum nangay natsun

My guru gave me only one advice—
from outside transfer the attention within.
That became Lallā's initiation—
that is why I began to wander naked.

51

असी आंसि तय अंसीय आसव
असिय दोर करि पतवथ
शिवस सोरि नु ज्योन तु मरुन
रवस सोरि नु अतगथ

asī äsi tay asīy āsav
asiy dor kari patavath
śivas sori na zyŏn ta marun
ravas sori na atagath

In the past we existed,
in the future we shall be,
and through the ages we have been.
Śiva continues to create and destory
just as the sun continues to rise and set.

52

दॅमी डीठम गज दॅज़ॅवॅनॅी
दॅमी इॅयूठुम दह नॅ तॅ नार
दॅमी डीठम पाण्डवन हन्ज़ मांजी
दॅमी डीठम क्रांजी मास

damī ḍīṭham gaj dazvanī
damī ḍyūṭhum dah na ta nār
damī ḍīṭham pāṇḍvan hanz mäjī
damī ḍīṭham kräjī mās

Just now I saw
a fire ablaze in the hearth.
And then I saw
neither smoke nor fire.
Just now I saw
the mother of Pāṇḍavas
and then I saw her
as the aunt in the potter's house.[15]

---

[15] This verse is a metaphor for the shifting fortunes in the material world. The reference here is specifically to the story of the Pāṇḍavas' fortune and misfortune in the Mahābhārata.

53

द्वादशान्त मंडल यस दीवस थजि
नासिक पवन दारि अनाहत रव
स्वयम कल्पन अंतिह त्रजि
पानय सु दीव त अर्त्तुन कस

dvādashānta maṇḍal yas dīvas thaji
nāsika pavana däri anāhata rav
svayam kalpan antih tsaji
pānay su dīv ta artsun kas

Whoever realizes *brahmarandhra* cakra
as the abode of the deity,
hears the all-pervasive,
unobstructed sound through breath control
and ends self-delusion,
she herself is the deity.
Then who should she worship?

5 4

कुस डिंगि त् कुस ज़ागि
कुस सर वतरि तेलिय
कुस हरस पूज़ि लागि
कुस परम्पद मेलिय

kus dingi ta kus zāgi
kus sar vatari teliy
kus haras pūzi lāgi
kus paramapad meliy

Who is asleep
and who is awake?
From which lake does water ooze out?
What can be offered in worship to god?
What supreme state
is to be attained?

55

मन डिंगि त॒ अक्वल ज़ागि
दांडय सर पंन्न॒-यंदि वतरि तेलिय
स्वव्यचार॒ पोञ हरस पूज़ि लागि
परम॒पद ऩीत॒न शिव मेलिय

man dingi ta akval zāgi
dädi sar pañtsa yandi vatari teliy
svavĕtsāra poñ haras pūzi lāgi
paramapad tsītan śiva meliy

Mind is asleep,
and the nameless Self is awake.
Five sense organs are the lake
from which water constantly oozes.
Self-introspection is the oblation to god.
Śiva consciousness
is the supreme state to be achieved

56

शिव गुर तय कीशव पल‍ुनस
ब्रह्मा पायर्यन वो‍लास्यस
यूगी यूग-कलि परज़ान्यस
कुस दीव अश्ववार प्यठ चडयस

śiva gur tay kīśava palanas
brahmā pāyrĕn vŏläsĕs
yūgī yūg kali parzānĕs
kus dīva ashvavār pĕṭh ceḍyĕs

Śiva is the horse,
Keśava is the saddle
and Brahmā is on the stirrups.
A yogi through yogic practice
recognizes the One
riding the horse.

57

अनाहत ख-स्वरूप शून्यालय
यस नाव न वरन न गुथर न रूप
अहं विमर्श नाद्-ब्यंद्य यस वो्न
सुय दीव अश्ववार प्यठ चडयस

anāhata kha-svarūp śūnyālay
yas nāv na varan na guthr na rūp
aham vimarśa nād-běnday yas vŏn
suy dīva ashvavār pět̄h cěḍěs

The unstruck sound of Om,[16]
all permeating,
whose abode is void,
without name,
colour, caste or form.
Self-introspection reveals
  the unsounded resonance.
That is the deity riding the horse.

---

[16] This specific Kashmīrī Śaiva practice involves developing focused attention through disengaging oneself from sensory perceptions, withdrawing within, and exercising breath control and silent absorption in the sound Om.

58

शिशिरस वुथ कुस रटे
कुस ब्वके रटे वाव
युस पाँछ यिंदरय च्यलिथ चटे
सुय रटे गटे रव

shishiras vuth kus raṭe
kus bŏke raṭe vāv
yus pāntsh yindray tsĕlith tsaṭe
suy raṭe gaṭe rav

Who can stop the drip from icicles?
Who can hold air in the palm?
She who controls the five sense organs
sees the sun in the darkness.

59

च्यत् तुर्ग गगन् ब्रमवोन
निमिशि अकि छन्डि यूज़न् लछ
च्यतनि वगि ब्वदि रॅटिथ ज़ोन
प्राण-अपान सन्दारिथ पख़ुच

tsĕta turg gagna bramavon
nimiśi aki tshaṇḍi yūzan lach
tsĕtani vagi bŏdi raṭith zon
prān-apān sandärith pakhac

The mind-horse wanders all over
with the flicker of an eyelid,
traveling a hundred thousand leagues.
Whoever holds the reins
with self-restraint and discrimination,
succeeds in controlling
the inhaled and the exhaled breath.

60

अब्यासी सव्यकास लय॒ वो॒थू
गग॒नस सगुन म्यूल समिन्न्रटा
शून्य गो॒ल त अनामय मो॒तू
युहो॒य वो॒प॑दीश छुय बटा

abyāsī savyakās laya vŏthū
gaganas sagun myūl samitsraṭā
śūnya gŏl ta anāmay mŏtū
yuhŏy vŏpadīsh chuy baṭā

Through constant practice,
the objective reality is withdrawn.
The world of forms and colors
suddenly merges with the void.
When the void disappears,
nameless consciousness remains.
This is my teaching, Paṇḍit!

61

न॒ न॒ बो॒ह न॒ देय न॒ द्यान
गौ पानय सर्वक्रिय मंशिथ
अन्यव ड्यूठुख कें॒छ॒ न॒ अन्वय
गंय सथ लयि पर पंशिथ

tsa na bŏh na deya na dyān
gav pānay sarva kriy maśith
anyav ḍyūṭhukh keṅtsh na anvay
gayi sath layi par paśith

Neither you nor I,
and neither meditation
nor the object of meditation exist.
The All-doer forgets Himself.
The blind find this meaningless.
The wise become one
with this supreme state.

62

द्यन छयज़ि त् रज़न आसे

बूतल गग्नस कुन व्यकासे

ऩ्न्दर राह ग्रो॒स माव॒से

शिव्-पूज़ुन गौ न्न्त्तात्मसे

dĕn tshĕzi ta razan āse

būtal gaganas kun vĕkāse

tsandar rāh grŏs māvase

śiva puzun gav tsittātmase

The day passes into the night.
The earth reaches out for the sky.
On the day of the new moon,
the moon swallows Rāhu.[17]
Śiva's worship is the realization
of the self as consciousness.

---

[17] Rāhu is the demon of eclipse in Indian mythology.

63

तूरि सलिल् खोत् तय तूरे
ह्यमि त्रे गय ब्योन-अब्योन व्यमर्शा
च्रैतन्य रव बाति सब समे
शिवमय च्रराच्रर जग पश्या

türi salila khŏta tay türe
hĕmi trĕ gay byŏn abyŏn vĕmarśā
tsaitani rav bāti sab same
śivamay tsarātsar zag paśya

Cold changes water into ice or snow.
Discernment shows the three different states
are not really different.
When the sun of consciousness shines,
the plurality is dissolved into oneness.
The universe appears throughout permeated
with Śiva.

64

शील त॒ मान छुय पोञ क्रंजे
म्वछि यमि रोट मलि यो॒द वाव
होस्त युस मस्त वाल गन्डे
ति यस तगि तय सु अद॒ न्यहाल

shīl ta mān chuy poñ kraṇje
mŏchi yami rot mali yŏd vāv
hosta yus mastavāl gaṇḍe
ti yas tagi tay su ada nĕhāl

Name and fame
are like water in a sieve.
Whoever has strength
to hold air in a fist
and tie an elephant
with a strand of hair
will certainly attain bliss.

The House of Nectar

65

छांडान लूसस पांनिय-पानस
छयपिथ ग्यानस वोतुम न् कूंछ्
लय कंरमस त् वांन्स अलथानस
बरि बरि बान् त् च्यवान न् कूंह

tshāṇḍān lūsas päniy pānas
tshĕpith gyānas votum na kuṅtsh
lay karmas ta vätsas althānas
bari bari bāna ta cĕvān na kūṅh

Arduous was my search for the Self.
Nothing compares to the hidden knowledge.
Self-absorption led me
to the house of nectar—
cups I found filled to the brim,
but nobody was drinking.

66

यि क्याह आंसिथ यि क्युथ रंग गोम
चंग गोम ऩटिथ हुद हुद॑न्यीय द॑गय
सारिनिय पदन कुनिय वखुन प्योम
ललि म्यं त्राग गोम लग॒ कमि शांठय

yi kyāh äsith yih kyuth rang gom
cang gom tsaṭith huda hudaněy dagay
sāriniy padan kunuy vakhun pyom
lalli mě trāg gom laga kami shāṭhay

What was I
and what has become of me?
My attachments are severed.
All verses echo only one thing.
I, Lallā, have become a lake.
Where shall I find my shore?

67

श्यं वन त्रटिथ शशिकल वुज़म
प्रक्रथ हन्ज़म पवन् सांती
लोलुकि नार् वालिंज बुज़म
शंकर लोबुम तमिय सांती

šĕ van tsaṭith šašikal vuzam
prakrath hanzam pavana sätī
lolaki nāra välinj buzam
šaṅkara lobum tamiy sätī

After traversing six forests,[18]
I awakened the orb of the moon.
By controlling my breath,
I gave up attachment to worldly things.
I roasted my heart
in the fire of love—
I found Śaṅkara that way.

_____

[18] The "six forests" refer to the six cakras or energy centers along the
spine— *mūlādhāra, svādhiṣṭhāna, maṇipura, anāhata, viśuddhā, ājñā*

68

मंकिरस ज्न मल न्रोलुम मनस
अद् म्यं लंबुम ज्नस ज्ञान
सुह यंलि ड्यूठुम निशि पानस
सोरुय सुय त् बोह नो केन्ह

makaris zan mal tsŏlum manas
ada mĕ labam zanas zān
suh yali ḍyūṭhum nishi pānas
soruy suy ta bŏh no keṅh

Impurities of my mind
were wiped away as from a mirror,
and I attained self-knowledge.
I saw him near me—
He is everything,
and I am nothing.

69

ललॎ बोॎह ऩायस स्वमनॎ बागॎबरस
वुछुम शिवस शक्थ मीलिथ तॎ वाह
तति लय कॎरॎम अमृतसरस
ज़िॅदय मरॅस तॎ म्यॅ करि क्याह

lalla bŏh tsāyas svamana bāgabaras
vuchum śivas śakath mīlith ta vāh
tati lay karam amritsaras
zinday maras ta mĕ kari kyāh

I, Lallā, entered the door
to the garden of my mind.
I saw Śiva and Śakti in communion.
I became immersed in the nectar of bliss.
I died while still alive—
nothing worries me.

70

मद प्यो्म स्यंदि ज्लन यूत
रंगन लीलमि कर्यम क्च
कंति ख्ययम मन्शि माम्सकि नली
स्वय बो्ह लल् त् गव म्यं क्याह

mad pyŏm syandi zalan yūt
rangan līlami karyam katsa
kati khyĕm manaśi māmasaki nalī
svay bŏh lalla ta gav mĕ kyāh

I drank wine as the water from Sindhu.
How many roles did I play on the world stage?
How many pieces of meat[19] did I eat?
I am still the same Lallā—
nothing happened to me.

---

[19] The third line of the Kashmīrī verse has an archaic expression whose
meaning has been lost. Its literal meaning "pieces of human flesh" does
not make sense in the context of Lallā's life and verses. Grierson inter-
prets the expression as a metaphor for human experience (p. 97).

71

नियम कर्योथ गर्बा
च्यतस कर्बा प्यंयी
मरन् ब्रोंठय मरबा
मरिथ त् मरतब् हरिय

niyam karyoth garbā
tsĕtas karbā pyĕy
marana bronṭhay marbā
marith ta martaba hariy

When will you remember
the vow you made in the womb?
Die before your death.
Then at death you will attain a higher state.

72

हा मनशि क्याज़ि छुख वुठान स्यकि लवर
अमि रटि हा मालि पंकिय न् नाव
ल्यूखुय यि नारांनि कर्मनि रांखि
ति मालि ह्यकिय न् फीरिथ कान्ह

hā manaśi kyāzi chukh vuṭhān sĕki lavar
ami raṭi hā māli pakiy na nāv
lyūkhuy yi nārāni karmani räkhi
ti māli hĕkiy na phīrith kāṅh

O, Fellow Being! Why are you twisting
a rope of sand?
By holding on to this rope,
my dear, the boat will not move.
Whatever god has written in your karma
nobody, my dear, can change.[20]

---

[20] The expression "twisting a rope of sand" refers to futile effort people engage in to achieve self-realization.

73

मन॑सय मान बव् सरस
छ्यूर् कूप नेरयस नारुख् छो॒ख
ल्यकां ल्यख युद् तुला को॒टि
तुलि तूल त तुल न केंह

manasay mān bavsaras
chyūr kūpa nerĕs nārukh chŏkh
lĕkä lĕkh yuda tulā kŏṭi
tuli tūl ta tul na keṅh

Consider your mind
an ocean of earthly existence.
If not restrained,
fiery words will burst out in anger.
If weighed on a scale,
these words have no mass.

74

केंह छिय न्यांद्रि हंती वुदी
केंज़न वुद्हन न्यसर प्यंयी
केंह छिय स्नान कंरिथ अपूती
केंह छिय गेह बज़िथ ति अक्रयी

keṅh chiy nyĕndrihatī vudī
keṅtsan vudĕn nĕsar pĕyī
keṅh chiy snān karith apūtī
keṅh chiy geh bazith ti akriyī

Some though asleep are awake,
some while awake have fallen asleep,
some are dirty after a bath,
and some even as householders
are totally detached.

75

ज्रल च्यत्ता वो॒न्दस बयि मो बर
चोन ज्रिथ करान पान् अनाद
च्यं॑ को ज़ननि ख्यो॒द हरि कर
कीवल तसुंदुय तारुक नाद

tsal tsĕttā vŏndas bayi mo bar

con tsinth karān pāna anād

tsĕ ko zanani khyŏd hari kar

kīval tasunduy tāruk nād

Fickle Mind,

don't be overcome by fear!

You are cared for

by the beginningless source.

You do not know

when your hunger is satiated.

Meditate only on

the all-permeating unobstructed sound.

76

यव् तूर ऋलि तिम अंबर ह्वता
ख्योद यव् गलि तिम आहार अन्न
च्यंत्ता स्व पर व्यंत्रारस प्यता
ऋेन्तन यि दीह वनकावन

yava tür tsali tim ambar hĕtā
khyŏd yava gali tim āhār ann
tsĕttā sva para vyĕtsāras pĕtā
tsentan yi dīh vankāvan

Wear the clothes
that protect you from cold.
Eat that food
which satisfies your hunger.
Mind, meditate on the Self.
Consider this body to be food
for forest ravens.

77

ख्यन् ख्यन् करान कुन नो वातख
न् ख्यन गछख अहंकारी
सो_मुय ख्यं मालि सो_मुय आसख
समि ख्यन् मुन्नरनय बरंन्यन तारी

khĕna khĕna karān kun no vātakh
na khĕna gatshakh ahankärī
sŏmuy khĕ māli sŏmuy āsakh
sami khĕna mutsaranay barñen tärī

Indulging in eating
will lead you nowhere.
By refraining from eating,
you will become egotistical.
By eating moderately,
you will achieve equanimity.
By practicing moderation,
the closed doors will be unbolted.

78

ख्यथ गण्डिथ शमि न॒ मानस
ब्रांथ यिमव त्रांव तिमय गय खसिथ
शास्त्र बूज़िथ छु यम॒ बय क्रूर
सु न॒ पो॒न्न त॒ दनी लसिथ

khĕth gaṇḍith shami na mānas
brānth yimav träv timay gay khasith
shāstra būzith chu yama bay krūr
su na pŏtsa ta danī lasith

Tranquility is not achieved
by only eating and clothing oneself.
Those who give up false hopes
attain their goal.
Listening only to scriptures
intensifies the fear of death.
Whoever does not lean on them flourishes.

79

अकुय ओमकार युस नाबि दरे
क्वम्बॖय ब्रह्माण्डस सुम गरे
अख सुय मन्थर च्यतस करे
तस सास मन्थर क्या करे

akuy oṃkār yus nābi dare
kŏmbay brahmāṇḍas sum gare
akh suy manthr tsĕtas kare
tas sās manthr kyā kare

Whoever holds an Oṃ in the navel,
and through breath control
raises it to *brahmarandhra*—
absorbed in only this mantra,
he has no need for other mantras.

80

ज़ल थमवुन हुतवह तूरनावुन
ऊर्ध्वगमन् पैरिव ञयथं
काठदेनि द्वद श्रमनावुन
अन्तिह सकलु कपठ ञयथं

zal thamavun hutvah türnāvun
ūrdvagamana pairiv tsarĕth
kāthadeni dvad shramnāvun
antih sakalu kapaṭh tsarĕth

Stopping the rain
and extinguishing the fire,
levitation
and milking a wooden cow—
in the end, all this is deceitful exhibition.

81

कलन काल् ज़ालि योदवय च्यं गोल
व्यन्दिव गेह व् व्यन्दिव वनवास
ज़ानिथ सर्वगथ प्रोबु अमोल
युथुय ज़ानख त्युथुय आस

kalan kāla zäli yŏdvay tsĕ gol
vĕndiv geh va vĕndiv vanvās
zänith sarvagath prŏbu amŏl
yuthuy zānakh tyuthuy ās

As your longings disappear,
whether you are a householder or a recluse,
you realize god as pure and all pervading.
What you perceive is what you will attain.

82

पर तय पान य्ंमि सोम मोन
य्ंमि ह्युह मोन द्यन क्योह राथ
य्ंमिसय अद्वय मन सां-युन
तमिय ड्ययूठुय सुरग्वरनाथ

par tay pān yĕmi sŏm mon
yĕmi hyuh mon dĕn kyoh rāth
yĕmisay advay man sänpun
tamiy ḍyūṭhuy suragvarnāth

Whoever experiences
the self and the other as equal,
the day and the night as the same,
and whoever frees the mind of duality,
has the vision of the lord of creation.

83

शिव छुय थलि थलि रोज़ान
मो ज़ान ह्योंद् त् मुसलमान
त्रुक अय छुख त् पान पनुन पर्ज़्नाव
स्वय छै साहिबस सांत्य ज़ानी ज़ान

śiva chuy thali thali rozān
mo zān hyŏnd ta musalmān
truk ay chukh ta pān panun parzanāv
svay chay sāhibas sätya zānī zān

Śiva is omnipresent.
Don't differentiate between
Hindus and Muslims.
If you are wise,
you will recognize your true Self—
that is your real acquaintance with the lord.

84

युह यि कर्म करि प्यतुरुन पानस
अर्जुन बर्जुन ब्ययिस क्युत
अन्तिह लागि-रोस्त् पुशिरुन स्वात्मस
अद् यूर्य गछ् त तूर्य छुम ह्योत

yuh yi karm kari pĕtarun pānas
arzun barzun bĕyis kyut
antih lāgi-rŏst puśirun svātmas
ada yūri gatsha ta tūri chum hyŏt

Responsibility for your actions
you must bear—
others share their fruits.
Without attachment,
I offer my actions to the Self.
Wherever I go is all right with me.

85

करम ज़ह कारन त्रेह क्वम्बिथ
यव लबख परलूकस आंख
वो॒थ खस सूर्यमंडल च्वम्बिथ
तवय ऩलिय मरऩन्य शांख

karam zah kāran treh kŏmbith
yava labakh paralūkas āṅkh
vŏth khas sūryamaṇḍal tsŏmbith
tavay tsaliy maranañi shāṅkh

Two types of actions
and three are the causes.[21]
Through *kumbhaka*,[22]
you will find the other world.
Arise, ascend
and pierce the sun's disc.
That is how you will lose the fear of death.

---

[21] The causes, leading to limited perception, are the three types of
impurities or *malas*—*āṇavamala, māyīyamala, karmamala.*

[22] *Kumbhaka* is a yogic practice of breath control.

86

यहै मात्रि-रूपि पय दिये
यहै बार्य रूपि करि विशीश
यहै माय् रूपि अन्ति जुव ह्वांये
शिव छुय क्रूठ त चेन वोप'दीश

yahai mātri-rūpi pay diye
yahai bārya rūpi kari viśīsh
yahai māya rūpi anti zuv hĕye
śiva chuy krūṭh ta tsen vŏpadīsh

As mother she suckles the child.
As wife she performs yet another role.
As *māyā*, she dissolves in the end.[23]
To attain Śiva is difficult –
heed my advice.

---

[23] The word "*māyā*" refers to the material world as an illusion.

87

कुस मरि तय कसू मारन

मरि कुस तय मारन् कस्

युस हर-हर त्रॉविथ गर गर करे

अद् सु मरि तय मारन तस

kus mari tay kasū māran

mari kus tay māran kas

yus hara hara trävith gara gara kare

ada su mari tay māran tas

Who will die
and who will be killed?
Who will it kill and who will kill it?
Whoever quits chanting "hara,"
and instead recites "gara," "gara"[24]
is the one who dies and the one who is killed.

---

[24] "Hara" is a term commonly used to refer to God Viṣṇu and "gara"
means "home" in Kashmīrī. In this verse, chanting "gara" refers to
one's preoccupation with worldly affairs.

88

ग्वर शब्दस युस यछ़ पछ़ बरे
ग्यान् वगि रटि च्यत् त्वर्गस
यन्द्रयै शोमृरिथ आनंद करे
अद् कुस मरि तय मारन कस

gvara shabdas yus yatsh patsh bare
gyāna vagi raṭi tsĕta tŏrgas
yandrai shŏmrith ānand kare
ada kus mari tay māran kas

Whoever trusts the guru's words
seizes the mind-horse
with the reins of knowledge.
Whoever controls the senses,
attains bliss.
Then who will die and who will be killed?

89

टयो॒ठ मो॒दुर तय म्यूठ ज़हर
यस युथ छुनुख जतन बाव
य॑मि यथ करुय कल त॒ कहर
सु तथ शहर वा॑तिथ प्यव

tyŏṭh mŏdur tay myūṭh zahr
yas yuth chunukh jatan bāv
yĕmi yath karuy kal ta kahar
su tath śahar vätith pĕv

Bitter is sweet
and sweet is poisonous.
Effort and single-minded devotion
determine the final achievement.

90

ज्ञालुन छु वुज़मल् त् त्रटय
ज्ञालुन छु मंदिन्यन गटकार
ज्ञालुन छु पान पनुन कडुन ग्रटय
ह्यंत् मालि सन्तूश वाती पानय

tsālun chu vuzmala ta traṭay
tsālun chu mandinĕn gaṭakār
tsālun chu pān panun kaḍun graṭay
hĕta māli santūsh vātī pānay

Endure lightning and thunder.
Endure darkness at noon.
Endure passing through the grinding mill.
If you are content, dear,
he will come to you.

91

यॅम्य लूब मन्मथ मद च्रूर मोरुन
वत् नाशि मा॑रिथ त् लोगुन दास
तॅमिय सहज़् ईश्वर गोरुन
तमिय सोरुय व्यो॒न्दुन स्वास

yĕmi lūb manmath mad tsūr morun
vata nāshi märith ta logun dās
tamiy sahaz īśvara gorun
tamiy soruy vyŏndun svās

Whoever kills greed, lust, and ego
and then serves people with humility,
yearns for an all pervading god
and perceives everything else as ashes.

92

शिव-शिव करान हम्स्-गथ स्वरिथ
रूज़िथ व्यवंहॉरि द्यन क्योह राथ
लागि रोस्त अद्वय युस् मन करिथ
तसि न्यथ प्रसन सुरग्वरनाथ

śiva śiva karān hamsa-gath svarith
rūzith vĕvahäri dĕn kyŏha rāth
lāgi-rŏst advya yus man karith
tasi nĕth prasan suragvarnāth

Whoever recites the name of Śiva
and meditates on *hamsa*,[25]
conducting worldly activities
day and night
and liberating his mind
from desires and duality,
always pleases the lord of creation.

---

[25] *Hamsa*, a breath control practice, is a basic meditation in the Śaiva tradition.

The wine of Lalla's Verses

93

संन्नसस न् सातस पन्नसस न् रुमस
सु मस म्यं ललि च्यव पननुय वाख
अंदरिम गटख रटिथ त् वोलुम
न्नटिथ त् द्युत्मस त॑तिय चाख

satsasas na sātas patsasas na rumas
su mas mě lalli cěv pananuy vākh
andarim gaṭakh raṭith ta volum
tsaṭith ta dyutmas tatiy cākh

I did not pause for the right moment.
I did not trust anything.
The wine I, Lallā, drank
was my own verses.
I caught the inner darkness,
gathered it
and tore it into shreds.

94

आयस ति स्योदुय त् गछ् ति स्योदुय
स्यंदिस होल म्यं कर्यम क्याह
बोह तस आंसंस आगुरय व्यंज़य
व्यंदिस त् व्यंदिस कर्यम क्याह

āyas ti syŏduy ta gatsha ti syŏduy
syadis hŏl mĕ karĕm kyāh
bŏh tas äsas āgaray vĕzay
vĕdis ta vĕndis karĕm kyāh

I came here directly
and I will return directly.
What can wickedness do
to my simple and honest nature?
I am known to the beginningless source.
As its acquaintance and loved one,
no harm can come to me.

95

वाख मानस क्वल अक्वल न॒ अते
छ्वपि मुद्रि अति ना प्रवीश
रोज़ान शिव-शकथ ना अते
म्वतियै कुँह त॒ सुय वो॒पंदीश

vākh mānas kval akval nā ate
tshvapi mudri ati nā pravīsh
rozān śiva śakath nā ate
mŏtiyay kuṅh ta suy vŏpadīsh

Speech or mind and
manifest or transcendent
have no existence there.
Yogic silence has no place there.
Śiva and Śakti don't live there.
Seek whatever is left—
that is my advice.

96

तंथर गलि तय मंथर म्वन्ने
मंथर गोल तय मोतुय च्यथ
च्यथ गोल तय कंहति ना कुने
शून्यस शून्याह मीलिथ गौ

tanthr gali tay manthr mŏtse
manthr gŏl tay motuy tsĕth
tsĕth gŏl tay keṅhti nā kune
śūnyas śūnyāh mīlith gav

When teachings disappear,
the mantra remains.
When the mantra disappears,
consciousness remains.
When consciousness disappears,
nothing remains.
Nothingness merges with nothingness.

97

अज़पा गायत्री हम्स् हम्स् ज़पिथ
अहम् त्रांविथ सुय अद् रठ
यंम्य त्रोव अहं सुय रूद पानय
बोह न् आसुन छुय वोपंदीश

azapā gāyatrī haṃsa haṃsa zapith
ahaṃ trävith suy ada raṭh
yĕmi trov ahaṃ suy rūd pānay
bŏh na āsun chuy vŏpadīsh

Recite *haṃsa* with every breath.
Renounce the self
and meditate on the Self.
Whoever renounces the self,
 finds the Self.
Negating the I-ness is my advice.

98

कन्दौ गेह त्यजि कन्दौ वनवास
व्यफो्ल मन न् रटिथ त् वास
द्यन राथ गंज॑रिथ पनुन श्वास
युथुय छुख त् त्युथुय आस

kanděv geh tězi kanděv vanvās
věphŏla man na raṭith ta vās
děn rāth ganzarith panun shvās
yuthuy chukh ta tyuthuy ās

Some renounce their home,
and some their hermitage.
All is futile
if the mind is not under control.
Meditate on your breath
day and night,
and stay wherever you are.

99

कुश पोश तेल दीफ जल ना गछे
सद्बाव् ग्वर्-कथ युस मनि ह्ाँये
शोम्बुहस स्वरि न्यथ पनंनी यंछे
सदा प्यज़े सहज़्-अक्रयी ना ज़्यये

kuś poś tel dīph zal na gatshe
sadbāva gvara-kath yusa mani hĕye
śŏmbuhas svari nĕth pananī yatshe
sadā pĕze sahaz-akriy na zyaye

No need for kuś grass, flowers,
sesame seeds, lamp, or water.
Whoever accepts the teacher's words
in simple faith
and remembers Śambhu[26] daily
of his own volition,
absorbed in all-pervasive unobstructed sound,
becomes liberated.

---

[26] Śambhu is a name for Śiva.

100

कुन्यरै बोज़ख कुनि नो रोज़ख
कुनिरन को॒रनम हंनीयाकार
कुनंय आसिथ द्वन हुन्द जंग गोम
सुय बेरंग गोम करिथ रंग

kunĕray bozakh kuni no rozakh
kuniran kŏrnam hanīyakār
kunay äsith dvan hund jaṅg gom
suy beraṅg gom karith raṅg

When you grasp non-duality,
you lose self-consciousness.
The experience of the unity in duality
has erased my self-consciousness.
Even though it is One,
the conflict from duality persists.
The colorless One
has dyed me in worldly colors.

101

गाल गंन्डिन्यम बोल पंडिन्यम
दपिन्यम तिय यस यिह रोऩ्ने
सहज़ क्वसमौ पूज़ कंरिन्यम
बोह अमुलांन्य त॒ कस क्याह म्वऩ्ने

gāl gaṇḍinĕm bol paḍinĕm
dapinĕm tiy yas yih rŏtse
sahaza kŏsmav pūz karinĕm
bŏh amläñi ta kas kyāh mŏtse

Let them call me names or lecture me.
Let them call me what they wish.
Let them offer me flowers of devotion.
I am untouched—
so who will gain by it?

102

सहज़स शम त॒ दम नो गछे
य॑छि नो प्रावख मुक्ति द्वार
सलिलस लवन ज़न मीलिथ गछे
तोति छुय द्रर्लब सहज़॒ व्यऩ्ऩार

sahazas sham ta dam no gatshe
yatshi no prāvakh mukti dvār
salilas lavan zan mīlith gatshe
toti chuy dvarlab sahaza vyĕtsār

For self-knowledge,
self-restraint and breath control
are not enough.
Liberation is not achieved
through wishing alone.
Though you are completely absorbed in the Self,
like salt dissolved in water,
it is still rare to know the truth about the Self.

103

ग्रट छु फेरान ज़ेरे ज़ेरे
ओ॒हुकुय ज़ानि ग्रटुक छ्ल
ग्रट यलि फेरि तय ज़ांव्युल नेरे
गू वाति पानय ग्रट्बल

graṭa chu pherān zere zere
ŏhukuy zāni graṭuk tshal
graṭa yali pheri tay zävyul nere
gū vāti pānay graṭabal

The grindstone moves
when set in motion.
The axle knows the mystery
of the grindstone.
When the grindstone moves,
fine flour comes out
as the wheat moves by itself
into the grindstone
to be crushed.[27]

---

[27] The working of the grindstone is a metaphor for human existence.

104

ज़ननि ज़ायाय रत्य तय कुतिय
कॅरिथ वो॒दरस बहु कलीश
फीरिथ द्वार बज़नि वात्य तु॒तिय
शिव छुय क्रूठ तय च्नेन वो॒पंदीश

zanani zāyäy ratiy tay katiy
karith vŏdaras bahu klīsh
phīrith dvār bazani vāti tatiy
śiva chuy krūṭh tay tsen vŏpadīsh

We are born
to the mother healthy and fit
after causing much suffering
when inside the womb.
Then we return and wait for the same door.
Attaining Śiva is difficult—
heed this advice.

105

अछ्यन आय त् गछुन गछे
पकुन गछे द्यन क्योह राथ
योरय आय त् तूर्य गछुन गछे
केंह नत् केंह नत् केंह नत् क्याह

atshĕn āya ta gatshun gatshe
pakun gatshe dĕn kyoh rāth
yoray āya ta tūri gatshun gatshe
keṅh nata keṅh nata keṅh nata kyāh

Birth and death
occur continually
as day and night
come and go.
From where we came,
we must return.
There is something to it.

106

त्रयि न्यंगि सराह सर्य सरस
अकि न्यंगि सरस अर्शस जाय
हरम्वख् कौंसर् अख सुम सरस
सति न्यंगि सरस शून्याकार

trĕyi nĕngi sarāh sari saras
aki nĕngi saras arśas jāy
harmŏkha kauṅsara akh sum saras
sati nĕngi saras śūnyākār

Three times I saw
the lake overflowing.
Once I saw
a place to step on to the sky.
Once I saw a bridge
from Harmukh to Kaunsar.
Seven times I saw
the manifest world vanish into the void.

107

सम्सारस आयस तपसी
बोद प्रकाश लोॢबुम सहज़
मरयम नॢ कान्ह तॢ मरॢ नॢ कॏसि
मरॢ नेछ तॢ लसॢ नेछ

samsāras āyas tapasī
boda prakāśa lŏbum sahaz
marĕm na kāṅh ta mara na kaṅsi
mara nech ta lasa nech

I came to this world a hermit.
Through meditation on the Self,
I attained the light of knowledge.
No one will die for me,
and I will die for nobody.
Life and death are the same.

108

यथ सरस सिरिफ़ोल न् व्यन्त्री
तथ सरि सकलंय पोज च्यंन
मृग सृगाल गण्डि जलहस्ती
ज्यन न् ज्यन त् तोतुय प्यंन

yath saras siriphŏl na vĕtsī
tath sari sakalay poñ cĕn
mrag sragāl gaṇḍi zalhastī
zĕn na zĕn ta tŏtuy pĕn

All drink from the lake
that can't hold
a grain of mustard.
Deer, jackal,
rhinoceros, and hippopotamus
arise from it
and fall into it.[28]

---

[28] The lake is a metaphor for the universal consciousness, which is the
source of the manifest world. Seen from the perspective of the universal consciousness, the manifest world is just an instant flash that
comes into existence and vanishes away.

109

लोलुक नार ललि ल्वलि ललनोवुम
मरनय म्वयस त॒ रूज़स न॒ ज़रै
रंगरछि॒ ज़ातसइ क्याह न॒ रंग होवुम
बो॒ह दपुन न्ंलुम क्याह सना करै

loluk nār lalli lŏlli lalanovum
maranay mŏyas ta rūzas na zarai
raṅgaratshi zātsay kyāh na raṅg hovum
bŏh dapun tsalum kyāh sanā karay

I, Lallā, suffered the fire of love.
Before death,
I died without a trace.
Born without color or creed,
what colors didn't I assume?
'I-ness' left me—
What else could I do?

Words of Wisdom

110

रावन् मंज़य रावुन रोवुम
रांविथ अथि आयस बवसरै
असान गिन्दान सहज़इ प्रोवुम
दपनुय कोरुम पानस सरै

rāvana manzay rāvun rovum
rävith athi āyas bavasarai
asān gindān sahaziy provum
dapanuy korum pānas sarai

In the midst of being lost,
I lost the sense of being lost.
After being lost,
I found myself in the worldly ocean.
Laughing and playing,
I attained the all-pervading Self—
this philosophy became a part of me.

111

दीव् वटा दीवर वटा
प्यठ् ब्वन् छुय यीक्वाठ
पूज़ कस करख हूट् बटा
कर मनस त् पवनस संगाठ

dīva vaṭā dīvar vaṭā
pĕṭha bŏna chuy yīkavāṭh
pūz kas karakh hūṭa baṭā
kar manas ta pavanas sangāṭh

The idol is stone,
and the temple is stone—
 all one from top to bottom
Who will you worship, learned Paṇḍit?
Learn to control your mind and your breath.[29]

---

[29] All stones come from the same earthly source irrespective of the function they serve. Similarly humans, Lallā says, come from the same source even though they belong to different castes, creeds, and classes.

112

कव् छुख दिवान अनिने बछ्
त्रुक अय छुक त् अंद॔र॒य अछ्
शिव छुय अ॔ति तय कुन मो गछ्
सहज़ कथि म्यानि करतो पछ्

kava chukh divān anine batsh
truk ay chuk ta andaray atsh
śiva chuy äti tay kun mo gatsh
sahaza kathi myāni karto patsh

Why are you groping like the blind?
If wise, you will turn your attention within.
Śiva is there.
No need to go anywhere else—
believe my simple words.

113

तल् छुय ज्युस तय प्यठ् छुख नऩ्ऩान
वनत् मालि मन क्यथ् पऩ्ऩान छुय
सोरुय सोॗम्बरिथ यति छुय म्वऩ्ऩान
वनत् मालि अन्न क्यथ् रोॗऩ्ऩान छुय

tal chuy zyus tay pyeṭha chukh natsān
vanta māli man kĕtha patsān chuy
soruy sŏmbrith yati chuy mŏtsān
vanta māli ann kĕtha rŏtsān chuy

Below you a pit
and above it you are dancing.
Tell me, my dear, how you can depend on it?
Everything you gather
is left behind.
Tell me, my dear,
how can you enjoy your meal?

114

क्याह बो़डुख मूह बव़संदरि दारे
सो़थ लूरिथ प्य'यिय तम पांख
यम़ बठ कऱनय कांल्य छोऱदारे
कव़ ज़न कासिय मऱनऩय शांख

kyāh bŏḍukh mūha bavasadri dāre
sŏth lūrith pĕyiy tam pāṅkh
yĕma baṭh karnay käli choradāre
kava zana kāsiy marnañi shāṅkh

Why are you immersed
in the sea of illusory pleasures?
Having destroyed the high banked road,
you are stuck in the mire.
At the appointed time,
death will take you.
Who will relieve you
of your fear of death?

115

मुडस ग्यानृच कथ नो व॒निज़े
खरस गोर दिन॒ राविय दोह
स्यकि शाठस ब्योल नो वविज़े
रावरिज़ि न॒ को॒म याज्यन तील

muḍas gyānac kath no vanize
kharas gor dina rāviy doh
sĕki shāṭhas byol no vavize
rāvrizi na kŏm yājĕn tīl

Don't talk to a fool about knowledge.
Giving molasses to a donkey
is a waste of time.
Don't plant seeds
in the sandy riverbank.
Don't waste oil on bran cakes.

116

प्रथ्य तीर्थन गछान सन्यास
गारान स्वदर्शन म्यूल
च्यत्ता पंरिथ मो न्यशपथ आस
डेशख दूरे द्रमुन न्यूल

prathay tīrthan gatshān sannyās
gārān svadarśan myūl
tsĕtta parith mo nĕshpath ās
ḍeśakh dūre dramun nyūl

A sanyasi goes to holy places
seeking self-knowledge.
Mind, in spite of learning,
don't be directionless—
from the distance, grass looks greener.

117

अव्यन्नार्य पोथ्यन छिहो मालि परान
यिथ् तोत् परान राम पंज्रस
गीता परान त् हीथा लबान
परंम गीता त् परान छयस

avĕtsäri pothĕn chiho māli parān
yitha tota parān rāma panjaras
gītā parān ta hīthā labān
param gītā ta parān chĕs

Those without discernment, my dear,
read religious books
as parrots recite "Rāma" in a cage.
Reading the Gītā becomes an excuse—
I have read the Gītā
and I am still reading it.

118

त्रेशि ब्वछि मो क्रेशिनावुन
यानि छययि तानि संदारुन दिह
प्रट चोन दारुन तॄ पारुन
कर वोॄपकारुन स्वय छय क्रिय

treśi bŏchi mo kreśināvun
yāni tshĕy tāni sandārun dih
phraṭ con dārun ta pārun
kar vŏpkārun svay chay kriy

Don't torture your body
with thirst and starvation.
When the body is exhausted,
take care of it.
Cursed be your fasts
and religious ceremonies.
Be good to others—
that is the real religious practice.

119

पवन पूरिथ युस अनि वगि
तस ब्वना स्पर्शि न ब्वछि त त्रेश
ति यस करुन अन्तिह तगि
संसारस सुय ज्यंयी नेछ

pavan pūrith yusa ani vagi
tasbŏna sparśi na bŏchi ta treś
ti yas karun antih tagi
samsāras suy zĕyī nech

Whoever controls the inhaled breath,
hunger and thirst do not touch him.
Whoever does this until the end
is born fortunate in the world.

120

राजस बांजि यम्य करतल त्यांजि
स्वर्गस बांजि छुय तफ तय दान
सहज़स बांजि यम्य ग्वर्-कथ पांजि
पाप्-प्वण्यु बांजि छुय पनुनुय पान

rajas bäji yĕmi kartal tyäji
svargas bäji chuy taph tay dān
sahazas bäji yĕmi gvara-kath päji
pāpa pŏñi bäji chuy panunuy pān

Whoever is a skilled swordsman
acquires a kingdom.
Whoever engages in penance and charity
goes to heaven.
Whoever follows the guru's words
gains self-knowledge.
He himself reaps the fruit of his good and bad
deeds.

121

मिथ्या कपठ असथ त्रोवुम
मनस कोरुम सुय वोपदीश
ज़नस अंदर कीवल ज़ोनुम
अनस ख्यनस कुस छुम दूश

mithyā kapaṭh asath trovum
manas korum suy vŏpadīsh
zanas andar kīval zonum
anas khĕnas kus chum düsh

I renounced
falsehood, deceit, and hypocrisy.
I told my mind to follow this teaching.
Only One I found in everyone—
what is wrong with eating with anyone?

122

जानह् नाडिदल मन् रंटिथ
ऩंटिथ वंटिथ कुटिथ कलीश
जानह् अद् अस्त् रसायन गंटिथ
शिव छुय क्रूठ त् ऩेन वो्पंदीश

zānaha nāḍidal man raṭith
tsaṭith vaṭith kuṭith klīsh
zānaha ada asta rasāyan gaṭith
śiva chuy krūṭh ta tsen vŏpadīsh

Had I known how to control
the inner channels—
how to cut them from desires
and how to guide them
to end my suffering—
then I would have made the elixir.
Śiva is difficult to attain, heed that advice.

123

कुस पुश त् क्वस् पुशांजी
कम कुसुम लांगिज्यस पूज़े
कमि गोड दिज्यस ज़ल्दांनी
कव् सन् मंथर् शंकर स्वात्म् वुज़े

kus puś ta kŏssa puśāñī
kam kusum lägizĕs pūze
kami gŏḍ dizĕs zaldäni
kava sana manthr śaṅkara svātma vuze

Who is the male florist and the female?
Which flowers should be offered for worship?
Which water should be used for anointing?-
Which mantra will awaken the Śaṅkara within?

124

मन पुश तय यछ पुशांजी
बार्वकि कुसुम लांगिज्यस पूज़े
शशिरस गो़ड दिज्यस ज़ल़दांनी
छ्वपि मंथऱ शंकर स्वात्म वुज़े

man puś tay yatsh pushäñi
bāvaki kusum lägizĕs pūze
shashiras gŏḍ dizĕs zaldäni
tshŏpi manthr śaṅkara svātma vuze

Mind is the male
and desire the female florist.
Offer the flowers of devotion in worship.
Anoint with the eternal nectar
dripping from the moon.
Silent recitation will awaken
the Śaṅkara within.

125

लूब मारुन सहज़ व्यन्नारुन
द्रोग ज़ानुन कल्पन त्राव
निशि छुय त॒ दूर मो गारुन
शून्यस शून्याह मीलिथ गव

lūb mārun sahaz vĕtsārun
drog zānun kalpan trāv
nishi chuy ta dūra mo gārun
śūnyas śūnyāh mīlith gav

Abandon desires
and meditate on the Self.
Realization is hard to achieve.
Stop daydreaming.
That is near you,
so don't search afar.
Nothingness merges with nothingness.

126

योसय शेल पीठस त पटस
सोय शेल छय प्रथिवुन दीश
सोय शेल शूबवुनिस ग्रटस
शिव छुय क्रूठ त त्सेन वोपंदीश

yŏsay shel pīṭhas ta paṭas
sŏy shel chay prathivun dīsh
sŏy shel shūbavanis graṭas
śiva chuy krūṭh ta tsen vŏpadīsh

The stone on the pedestal
and the pavement
is the same stone that comes from the earth.
The same stone adorns the grindstone.
To attain Śiva is hard—
heed my advice.

127

ज्रर्मन ज्रटिथ दितिथ पॅनि पानस
त्युथ क्या व्ययोथ त॒ फलिहि सोव
मूडस वो॒पॅदीश गय रींज़ि दुमटस
कनि दान्दस गोर आपरिथ रोव

tsarman tsaṭith ditith pani pānas
tyuth kyā vŏyoth ta phalihi sov
mūḍas vŏpadīsh gay rīnzi dumaṭas
kani dāṅdas gor āparith rov

On removing the skin,
you stretched it with pegs around yourself.
What did you sow
to have produced this fruit?
Giving advice to a fool
is like throwing pebbles at a dome
or milking a brown bull
after feeding it molasses.[30]

---

[30] Lallā expresses in this verse the futility of teaching spiritual discipline to people who are immersed in the material world. Such people reduce themselves to their bodies (hide), stretching it and anchoring it in the material world through pegs of desire.

128

रव मत् थलि थलि तांपितन
तांपितन वो॒त्तम वो॒त्तम दीश
वरुन मत् लूक् गर् अंन्नितन
शिव छुय क्रूठ तय न्नेन वो॒पंदीश

rav mata thali thali tāpitan
tāpitan vŏttam vŏttam dīsh
varuṇa mata lūka gara ätsitan
śiva chuy krūṭh tay tsen vŏpadīsh

Doesn't the sun shine everywhere
instead of shining only on good places?
Doesn't Varuṇa[31]
enter every house?
Attaining Śiva is difficult—
heed this advice.[32]

---

[31] Varuṇa is an important Vedic God associated with rain, rivers, and oceans.
[32] Lallā assures people of different castes, classes, and creeds that they are equally capable of acquiring self-knowledge since Śiva permeates both the inner and outer reality.

129

अथ मबा त्रावुन खर बा
लूक हन्ज़ क्वंग वार ख्येयिय
तति कुस बा दारीय थरबा
यति नुनिस कर्तल प्येयिय

atha maba trāvun khar bā
lūka hanz kŏng vär khĕyiy
tati kus bā dārīy thar bā
yati nanis kartal pĕyiy

Don't let your donkey loose.
It will graze
on other people's saffron fields.
Who but you will have
to bare your back there
to take sword strikes
when discovered.[33]

---

[33] The "donkey" in the verse refers to the mind. If the mind is not under control, it will engage in misdeeds for which the owner must suffer punishment. This verse says metaphorically that one must bear the fruits of one's actions.

130

मूडो क्रय छय न् दारुन त् पारुन
मूडो क्रय छय न् रंछिनि काय
मूडो क्रय छय न् दिह सन्दारुन
सहज़ व्यंन्नारुन छुय वो॒प॑दीश

mūḍo kriy chay na dārun ta pārun
mūḍo kriy chay na rachini kāy
mūḍo kriy chay na dih sandārun
sahaz vĕtsārun chuy vŏpadīsh

Fool, the right action is not
fasting and perfoming rituals.
Fool, the right action is not
protecting your body.
Fool, the right action is not
maintaining your body.
Meditation on the Self is my advice.

131

ग्यानॖमार्ग छय हाकॖ वॉर
दिज्यस शमॖ-दमॖ क्रिंय पोञ
लामात्रक्र पोश प्रानि-क्रंयि दॉर
ख्यनॖ ख्यनॖ म्वन्निय वॉरय छंन्य

gyāna mārg chay hāka vär
dizĕs sham dam kriyi poñ
lāmātsakra posh prāni kriyi där
khĕna khĕna mŏtsiy väray chĕn

The path of wisdom
is like a kitchen garden.
Nurture it with
self-restraint, tranquility, and good deeds.
Fruits of old deeds must be paid off
like the animal offered to the goddess.
Eating continuously from the garden
will clear it of the fruits of past deeds.

132

लज़ कासिय शीत न्यवारिय

तृन ज़ल करान आहार

यि कंम्य वो॒पंदीश को॒रुय हूट॒ बटा

अन्नीतन वटस सन्नीतन कठ द्युन आहार

laz kāsiy shīt něvariy

trina zala karān āhār

yi kami vŏpadīsh kŏruy hūṭa baṭā

atsītan vaṭas satsītan kaṭh dyun āhār

It covers your body
and protects you from cold.
It lives on grass and water.
Who gave you the advice, foolish Paṇḍit,
to offer a living sheep
to a lifeless stone?

133

ह्यथ कंरिथ राज्य फेरिना
दिथ कंरिथ त्रप्ति न‍ मन
लूब व्यना ज़ीव मरिना
ज़ीवन्त‍ मरि तय सुय छुय ग्यान

hĕth karith rāji pherina
dith karith träpti na man
lūba vĕna zīv marina
zīvanta mari tai suy chuy gyān

Acquiring a kingdom
will not make you content.
Renouncing it
will not satisfy your mind.
Free from desires,
you will not die.
Self-knowledge is to be dead
to worldly things while still alive.

134

मारुख मार्बूथ काम-क्रूद-लूब
नत् कान बंरिथ मारनय पान
मनय ख्यन दिख स्वव्यन्नार् शम
विशय तिहुंद क्याह-क्युथ दोर् ज्ञान

mārukh mārabūth kām krūd lūb
nata kān barith mārnai pān
manay khĕn dikh svavĕtsāra sham
viśay tihund kyāh kyuth dŏr zān

Kill your mortal enemies—
lust, anger, and desire.
Otherwise they would kill you with their arrows.
Calm them with self-restraint and good thoughts.
Recognize their nature and their power.

135

मूड ज्ञानिथ पशिथ त कोर
कोल श्रुतवोन ज़डरूपि आस
युस यी दपिय तस तीय बोल
योहय तत्व व्यंदिस छुह अब्यास

mūd zänith paśith ta kor
köl shrutavon zaḍa rūpi ās
yus yī dapiy tas tīya bol
yohay tattva vĕdis chuh abyās

Act ignorant, even if you know.
Act blind, even if you see.
Act dumb, even if you hear.
In short, act detached.
Whatever people tell you,
listen and agree.
This practice will lead to knowledge.

136

वो॒थ रां॑न्या अर्चुन सखर
अथि अल पल वखुर ह्यथ
योदवनय ज़ानख परम॒पद अखयर
हिशिय खो॒श ख्वर क्यथ ख्यथ

vŏth ränyā artsun sakhar
athi alpal vakhur hĕth
yodavanay zānakh paramapad akhĕr
hishiy khŏśa khŏr kĕtha khĕth

Arise, Lady! Prepare for worship
with wine, meat, and a dainty choice of food.
If you know the supreme state,
breaking customs will make no difference.

137

दछिनिस ओ॒बरस ज़ायुन ज़ानं॒ह॒
समुद्रस ज़ानं॒ह॒ कंडिथ अठ
मन्दिस रूगियस वैद्युत ज़ानं॒ह॒
मूडस ज़ा॑निम न॒ पृणित कथ

dachinis ŏbras zāyun zānaha
samudras zānaha kaḍith aṭh
mandis rūgiyas vaidyut zānaha
mūdas zänim na priñit kath

I may know how to
scatter southern clouds,
dry up an ocean,
or cure a chronically sick person,
but I never knew how to convince a fool.

138

मॉरिथ पांछ बूथ तिम फलहंडी
ञ्जीतन दान् त् वखुर ख्यथ
तदै ज्ञानख परम्पद त्ंडी
हिशी खो़श ख्वर कोति न् ख्यथ

märith pāñtsh būth tim phalhandī
tsītana dāna ta vakhur khĕth
taday zānakh paramapad tsaṇḍi
hishi khŏśa khŏr koti na khĕth

Kill the five elements of experience[34]
on a diet of meditation
and realize the supreme state—
breaking customs
makes no difference.

---

[34] The five elements of experience (*pañca-mahābhūtas*) of the physical world are solidity, aeriality, vacuity, liquidity, and formativity.

139

कन्द्यो करख कन्दि कन्दे
कन्द्यो करख कन्दि विलास
बूग॒य मीठि दितिथ यथ कन्दे
अथ कन्दि रोज़ि सूर न॒ त॒ सास

kandyo karakh kandi kande
kandyo karakh kandi vilās
būgay mīthi ditith yath kande
ath kandi rozi sūr na ta sās

Hey, you, preoccupied with your body.
Hey, you, busy adorning your body
and using it for sweet pleasures—
not even dust and ashes will remain of this body.

140

स्वमन् गारुन मंज़ यथ कन्दे
यथ कन्दि दपान स्वरूप नाव
लूब मूह च्नलिय शूब यियि कन्दे
यथि कन्दि तीज़ तय सोर प्रकाश

svamana gārun manz yath kaṇde
yath kandi dapān svarūp nāv
lūb mūh tsaliy shūb yiyi kande
yathi kandi tīz tay sor prakāśa

Seek the Self in the body.
This body is known as the abode of the Self.
Forsaking greed and attachment
will brighten the body.
The body will shine like the sun.

141

च्यथ अमरपथि थाविज़ि
ति त्राविथ लगिय ज़ूरे
तति च़ नो शीक्यज़ि संदारज़ि
द्वदशुर त् क्वछ नो मूरे

tsĕth amarapathi thävizi
ti trävith lagiy zūre
tati tsa no śikizi sandärizi
dvadashur ta kŏcha no mūre

Focus your attention on the immortal path.
If the mind strays from the path,
it will be lost.
Don't be afraid there—
be calm.
A suckling baby is quiet in the lap.

142

ज्ञामर छत्र रथ सिंहासन
ह्लाद नांटिरस तूल-परयांख
क्याह मांनिथ यंति स्थिर आसव्रुन
कव् ज़न कांसिय मरन्न्य शांख

tsāmar chathr ratha simhāsan
hlād nāṭiras tūla paryāṅkh
kyāh mänith yĕti sthir āsavun
kavzana kāsiy maranañi shāṅkh

A fly-whisk, a sunshade,
a chariot, and a throne.
Merry making, pleasures of theater,
or a soft bed—
which of these will endure here?
How can they relieve you
of the fear of death?

143

राज़ हंस आसिथ सपदुख को॒लय
कुस्ताम त्रो॒लुय क्याहताम ह्ब्थ
ग्रट॒ गव बंद तय ग्रटन ह्यो॒त गो॒लुय
ग्रट॒वोल त्रो॒लुय फल॒ फोल ह्ब्थ

rāza hams äsith sapadukh kölay
kustām tsoluy kyāhtām hĕth
graṭa gav band tay graṭan hyot gŏluy
graṭavol tsoluy phal phol hĕth

Even though a royal swan,
you have become mute.
Someone has run away with something.
As soon as the mill stopped,
the grain channel got choked.
The miller ran away with the grain.[35]

---

[35] The word *haṃsa* refers to the basic meditation in the Śaiva tradition involving breath control, and, literally, it refers to the bird "swan," often associated with beauty. This verse is a metaphor for spiritual experience.

144

अस प्वन्दि ज्वसि ज़ामि
न्यथय स्नान करि तीर्थन
वहर्य वांहरस नो_नुय आसि
निशि छुय त_ परज़ानतन

asi pŏndi zvasi zāmi
nĕthay snān kari tīrthan
vahari vāharas nŏnuy āsi
nishi chuy ta parzāntan

Laughing, sneezing, coughing, and yawning,
bathing daily at holy places,
revealed throughout the year—
That is near you,
so recognize it.

145

शिव छुय ज़ाव्युल ज़ाल वहरांविथ
क्रंज़न मंज़ छुय तरिथ क्यथ
ज़िंद नय वुछहन अद् कति मरिथ
पान मंज़ पान कड व्यत्ज़ांरिथ क्यथ

śiva chuy zävyul zāl vaharävith

kranzan manz chuy tarith kyath

zinda nay vuchahan ada kati marith

pāna manz pān kad větsärith kyath

Śiva is like a fine net spread everywhere,
subtly permeating the physical world.
If you don't see him while alive,
how can you do so when dead?
Through self-introspection,
remove the self from within yourself.

146

रंगस मंज़ छुय ब्योन ब्योन लबुन
सोरुय ऋालख बरख स्वख
ऋख रंश त वैर गालख
अद डेशख शिव सुंद म्वख

rangas manz chuy byŏn byŏn labun
soruy tsālakh barakh svakh
tsakh raśa ta vair gālakh
ada deshakh śiva sund mŏkh

The world is full of differences.
If you are tolerant,
you will be happy.
If you renounce anger, hate, and animosity,
you will see Śiva's face.

Appendix

Lallā and the Kashmīrī Śaiva Tradition

Lallā's verses tell the story of her spiritual journey as a Śaiva mystic. Her interest in the Kashmīrī Śaiva practice was deepened due to her disenchantment with the conditions of her material existence. Siddha Śrīkaṇṭha initiates her into Śaiva yoga and she strives to establish her own inner connection with the tradition based on her experience. As she advances in her practice, she is said to have surpassed even her teacher.

For a context for understanding Lallā's verses, I provide here a brief overview of the Kashmīrī Śaiva tradition.[1] Kashmīrī Śaivites view the ultimate reality as pure consciousness. Various terms, vibration (*spanda*), Self-awareness (*vimarśa*), and power (*bala*) are used to describe the activity of the universal consciousness, which is pure light (*prakāśa*), independent and unconditioned. The *prakāśa-vimarśamaya* nature of the universal consciousness makes it creative, dynamic, and active as it manifests itself in the diversity of the world.

The expansion of the universal consciousness results in the unfolding (*unmeṣa*) of the phenomenal world, and its contraction or infolding (*nimeṣa*) leads to the withdrawal of diversity into the unity of its original state. The metaphor of ocean and waves is used to describe the activity of the

---

[1] Kashmīrī Śaiva literature can be divided into three categories: a. *Āgama Śāstra* which includes among others tantras like the *Mālanīvijaya, Svacchanda, Vijñānabhairava, Mṛgendra, Rudryāmala, Netra*, and the *Śiva Sūtra* with its various commentaries b. *Spanda Śāstra* includes the *Spandakārikā* with various commentaries c. *Pratyabhijñā śāstra* includes Somānanda's *Śivadṛṣṭi*, Utpaladeva's *Īśvarapratyabhijñā*, Kshemarāja's *Pratyabhijñāhṛdaya*, and Abhinavagupta's *Tantrāloka* and *Tantrasāra* (Chatterji 128-169).

universal consciousness—the ocean symboilizes the universal
or Śiva consciousness and the waves the diversity of
the phenomenal reality. Just as waves emerge from the
vastness of the ocean, so it is with the individual
consciousness emerging from the Śiva consciousness, which
is the essential ground of both the manifest and the
unmanifest reality.

The activity of consciousness gives rise to three different
states: deep sleep, dreaming, and waking. Deep sleep
represents the state of unity in which the universal and the
individual consciousness coincide. The awareness of this
unity in deep sleep is merely unconscious, but if conscious
awareness of this unity exists, then it is called the "fourth
state" which is achieved through introspective contemplation.
The dream state represents the sphere of inner speech,
populated by thoughts and images that do not arise from
direct interaction with the outer world as in the waking state.
The dream state is thus unique to each individual as it is a
part of his or her subjective awareness. In the waking state,
as opposed to the dream state, the objective sphere
predominates and it is characterized by a sharp distinction
between the subject and the world of objects familiar to all.

Since the universal consciousness is the substratum of the
diverse phenomenal world, starting from humans at the top
of the evolutionary ladder down to the simplest non-living
matter, liberation lies in realizing one's own nature
(*svasvabhāva*), which is pure consciousness.

The *Spandakārikā*,[2] a poetic and semi-philosophical text,
summarizes the teachings contained in the *Śiva Sūtra*.
Utpaladeva's *Īśvarapratyabhijñā*, on the other hand, is a

---

[2] The *Spandakārikā* consist of fifty-three verses. Its authorship is
disputed. Some claim that this text was composed by Vasugupta or
revealed to him, while others insist that it is the work of his student
Kallaṭa.

systematization of *pratyabhijñā* philosophy.[3] According to
the *pratyabhijñā* philosophy the universal consciousness is
the source of creation, persistence, and withdrawal of the
universe. Comparing the *pratyabhijñā* and *spanda*
perspectives, Dyczkowski writes "while the *Pratyabhijñā*
stresses transcendence without ignoring or minimizing
immanence, *Spanda* stresses immanence grounded in
transcendence" (*The Stanzas* 193). This distinction is
important to remember as we explore Lallā's thought since
she shows a leaning toward the *pratyabhijñā* perspective and
seems to emphasize transcendence, but unlike it, ignores
the significance of immanence. This attitude is also reflected
in her austere lifestyle and her approach to her bodily needs.
The body is only important as long as it serves as a means to
bring her the experience of transcendence.

The *Spandakārikā* describe three types of impurities
(*āṇavamala, māyīyamala, and karmamala*), which lead to
limited vision and thus prevent the individual from realizing
her own nature. The *āṇavamala* is the metaphysical
ignorance that makes the individual experience herself as
limited. The *māyīyamala* makes the limited individual forget
her essential nature. The *karmamala* leads to the performance
of both good and bad deeds that leave impressions, which
further bind the individual to the material world. The

---

[3] The first philosophic treatise on Kashmīr Śaivism, *Śivadṛṣṭi*, was
composed by Somānanda toward the end of the eighth century. His
disciple Utpaladeva wrote *Īśvarapratyabhijñā*, the source text for
pratyabhijñā philosophy that was developed in Kashmīr between the
middle of the 9th and the 11th centuries. Both Abhinvavgupta (10th
century) and Kṣemarāja (11th century) wrote commentaries on
Īśvarapratyabhijñā. Kashmīrī Śaiva philosophy reached its pinnacle
in the hands of Abhinavagupta who brought about a syncretism of
different Śaiva schools in his voluminous *Tantrāloka*, a summariza-
tion of the *Tantrāloka* in *Tantrasāra*, a commentary on the *Parātrīmśikā*
and several other works. His work developed Trika Śaivism into an all
encompassing system, which is considered to be synonymous with
Kashmīrī Śaivism.

unenlightened remain unaware of their own nature, and hence, are bound by the limited vision of the empirical consciousness that confines them to the world of thoughts and ideas related to the objects of the world of senses.

The three powers associated with Śiva are: action (*kriyāśakti*), will *(icchāśakti)*, and knowledge *(jñānaśakti)*. The power to act (*kriyāśakti*) thus lies in the *spandāśakti* of Śiva, which is one's own essential nature. The *Śiva Sūtras* elaborate on the means of liberation and divide them into three categories: *śāmbhavopāya, śāktopāya*, and *āṇavopāya*. In the *śāmbhavopāya* the experience of self-realization occurs as a sudden flash of intuition revealing one's own nature as the source of both the outer world of diversity and the inner world of thoughts and speech. The *śāktopāya,* also called *jñānayoga,* involves focused examination of the nature of self. It is comprised of two types of practices—contemplation on the five-fold activity of Śiva (creation, persistence, destruction, concealment, and grace) and purification of one's thought constructs. By watching the rise and fall of thoughts in a state of passive alertness, the individual experiences one's grounding in the universal consciousness. Finally, the *āṇavopāya* involves focusing attention on one's body, breath, ritual, mantra, and so on. Eventually, all these practices lead to the realization that phenomenal reality emerges out of the ceaseless activity of the universal consciousness.

Lallā's approach to her practice can be classified under the *āṇavopāya*. She begins as a limited individual (*aṇu*) deeply attached to sense objects. In this state, she strongly identifies with her ego-consciousness. Some of Lallā's verses deal with the early stages of her practice when she feels overwhelmed by the conditions of her material existence. She searches for means to overcome her limited vision that binds her to the material reality. According to the *Śiva Sūtras* the individual consciousness is imprisoned in the world created out of thought constructs. The self gets attached to these constructs and on becoming attached, it is affected by states of pleasure and pain that leave behind impressions, thus further binding the self to the world that appears divided and separate. In the early stages of her quest, Lallā strives for detachment and equanimity in the face of ridicule she suffers from members of her community as she sets out on her own path. Thus, she says:

> Both good and bad, I must endure.
> My ears don't hear,
> and my eyes don't see.
> When the inner Self
> awakens in my heart,
> the lamp will shine
> even in the midst of a tornado. (V 9)

The first step toward self-knowledge, then, involves getting rid of the ego consciousness or I-ness and opening up to the Śiva consciousness. Also, focusing on the transitoriness of material things can be used as an aid to turning one's attention away from sense objects. Whereas in the *bhakti* tradition external deity and objects of worship are used to gain spiritual experience, in the Śaiva tradition external objects of worship are replaced by sustained contemplation on the Self. Since the attention constantly slips out of five sense organs, extreme will power must be cultivated to proceed with the practice. Lallā says:

> What will I do
> with the five, the ten, and the eleven?
> They have all emptied out the cauldron.
> If all had come together
> and pulled the rope,
> the eleven would not have lost the cow. (V 16)

The "five" in the above verse are the five principles (*pañca-mahābhūtas*) of experience of the physical world (solidity, aeriality, vacuity, liquidity, and formativity), the "ten" are the five organs of sense perception (*jñānendriyas*)

and the five of action (karmendriyas) and the "eleven" refer
to these ten with the mind (manas) arising from ego
consciousness (ahaṃkāra). Lallā comments here about the
necessity of emptying of the body, depicted as a cauldron, as
sense organs, along with organs of action, as well as the
mind, continually disperse one's attention. Consequently, the
experience of Śiva consciousness, represented by the "cow,"
is lost. If all are brought under control, self-knowledge can
be achieved.

Many of Lallā's verses deal specifically with the use of
breathing exercises to achieve a state of inner focus when
the activities of the body, mind and senses are brought to
rest. Controlling the mind and the senses is done through
the mastery of breathing. A few of Lallā's verses deal with
the actual practice in the Kashmīrī Śaiva tradition that
involves controlling the prāṇaśakti or vital breath:

> After wandering in ten directions,
> I found the true path.
> Through breath control,
> I penetrated the void—
> Śiva I saw permeating all.
> Shutting the six and the three,
> I found Śiva the root cause of all. (V 33)

This method of meditation involves focusing within,
watching the inhalation (apāna) and exhalation (prāṇa)
which is combined with the cessation of all thoughts. The
"six" in this verse refer to the five organs of senses and the
mind and the "three" refer to three body openings—all these
are brought to rest through introspection. The Vijñānabhairava gives innumerable techniques for this purpose. And
one of them is haṃsah, which involves meditation on the
middle space between the in-breath and out-breath. Fixing
one's attention on the space between two thoughts is yet
another extension of this practice. Instead of moving from
thought to thought, the practitioner focuses on the space
between two thoughts to experience the ground

from which all thoughts arise. Through constant absorption
in *hamsah*, the Self or Śiva is experienced as the essential
nature of both the outer world of diversity and the inner
world of the contemplating self.

> Recite *hamsa* with every breath.
> Renounce the self
> and meditate on the Self.
> Whoever renounces the self,
> finds the Self.
> Negating the I-ness is my advice. (V 97)

Lallā also refers to yet another practice that deals with
one's absorption in the sound of Om.[4] Lillian Silburn writes
that Lallā's references to Om can actually be traced to a
practice given in the *Svacchandatantra*, which describes the
ascent of the vital breath through the psychic centers of the
body while Om is sounded. The three syllables of the sounding
of Om, A, U, and M, are associated with psychic centers
located in the heart, throat, and the vault of the palate
respectively.[5] Regarding this practice, Lallā says:

While tracing the history of Om in India, Mark Dyczkowski writes
that in Vedic times Om was recited in the beginning of the Vedic
hymns and regarded as the male seed that fertilized the female hymn.
In Upaniṣidic times, the three syllables of the sound Om, AUM, came
to symbolize three states of consciousness—waking, dreaming, and
deep sleep. In the tantric literature, this symbolism is extended even
further in that the resonance at the end of the sounded AUM itself is
seen to incorporate subtler levels of awareness which are divided into
different phases: the half moon (*ardhacandra*), the point (*bindu*), the
limit (*nirodhikā*), the sound (*nāda*), the unstruck sound (*nādānta*),
the energy (*śakti*), the pervasive (*vyāpinī*), the equal one (*samāna*)
and the transmental (*unmanā*) (*The Stanzas* 252).

[5] The awakening of *kuṇḍalinī* and experiencing its ascent up the spine
to the *sahasrāra* constitutes the fundamental practice of Kashmīrī
Śaivism. See Silburn.

Doors and windows of my body I closed.
The prāna-thief I caught
and brought under control.
I tied it inside the chamber of my heart.
I whipped it with the syllable Oṃ. (V 27)

The three syllables AUM are also associated with three
states of consciousness—waking, dreaming, and deep sleep
and the three deities, Brahmā, Viṣṇu, and Rudra (a form of
Śiva). Lallā's verses do not give actual techniques, but rather
use metaphorical language to convey her own experiences
of higher states of awareness, which cannot be contained in
the reality assigned to the deities Brahmā, Viṣṇu, and Śiva
—the creator, the preserver and destroyer of the universe,
according to Hindu mythological literature. Thus, Lallā says:

Śiva is the horse,
Keśava is the saddle
and Brahmā is on the stirrups.
A yogi through yogic practice
recognizes the One
riding the horse. (V 56)

The unstruck sound of Oṃ,
all permeating,
whose abode is void,
without name,
colour, caste or form.
Self-introspection reveals
the unsounded resonance.
That is the deity riding the horse. (V 57)

Lallā's mastery of various breathing practices is indicated
by the legend that describes her teacher's amazement at the
intensity of her austerity during the forty-day fast of
candrāvana. On the full moon day, she enters a clean room,
stands in an earthen pot and covers her head with another
such pot. As the moon wanes, her body diminishes in size,
until on the fifteenth day the two pots, the top and the bottom,

join each other. Śrīkaṇṭha, her teacher, lifts the lid and sees trembling quicksilver inside. As the moon waxes, Lallā's body begins to increase in size until on the full-moon day she regains her old size. He is impressed by her performance and says that the disciple has overtaken the teacher (*gav tsāth gvaras kha'sith*) (Koul 1921, 312).

The above legend symbolically represents the essence of Kashmīrī Śaiva teachings. The recurrent cosmic cycles, the rising and setting of the sun and the moon, are self-perpetuating processes that are integrally related to the individual perception of these processes. The rising and falling of cosmic cycles as well as individual moments of cognition and perception represent the expansion (*unmeṣa*) and contraction (*nimeṣa*) of consciousness. The five-fold functions of Śiva (creativity, persistence, withdrawal, grace, and obscuration) are repeated in a limited way at the individual level as one engages in activities of cognition and perception. On the individual level, however, the powers of universal consciousness become a means of bondage. As Kashmīrī Śaiva texts point out, it is the obscuration power of Śiva that leads to the diversity of the world. Those who get entangled in this diversity without discovering its grounding in universal consciousness remain ignorant about the continuity between the subjective reality of the inner world and the objective reality of the outer world.

Whereas the first three functions of Śiva, creativity, persistence, and withdrawal, occur at both cosmic and individual level, the last two, grace and obscuration, are intimately tied to the individual striving to realize one's own nature (*svasvabhāva*). On the individual level, the moment of creation arises out of mental perceptions as one's attention is focused on inner objects of thought or external objects of perception. The enjoyment of the object of attention is the moment of persistence. And as the objective sphere is absorbed in pure consciousness and it lies there as if in a potential form, it is the moment of withdrawal. The objects of mental perception and cognition, if not withdrawn

completely into consciousness, leave behind impressions,
resulting in concealment or obscuration of the true nature
of reality. In this state, the objective reality is experienced as
separate and disconnected from oneself. The moment of
grace (*anugraha*) is marked by the realization that
underlying both the subjective and the objective sphere is
the universal consciousness that is one's own nature.

In the above legend, the transformation of Lallā's body
into a ball of vibrating quicksilver symbolically represents
her introspective state as she experiences expansion of her
consciousness. Lallā's body does not dissolve into the
blankness of nothingness, but is turned into vibrant
quicksilver, a metaphor for the higher state of consciousness,
also called the fourth state. The image presents the
immanence and transcendence in tension, leading to the
experience of the third space, which goes beyond the binary
dualism. In this state, the distinction between the subject
and the object disappears and the empirical consciousness
transcends the objective reality.

Transgressing the distinctions between the inside and
outside or the subject and object leads to the opening up of
an entirely new space that refuses to be contained in any
dualistic conceptual frameworks. The most profound of
Lallā's verses, then, try to represent just such an experience
which is unrepresentable since it goes beyond all thought
constructs, dualities, names and attributes.

> Speech or mind and
> manifest or transcendent
> have no existence there.
> Yogic silence has no place there.
> Śiva and Śakti don't live there.
> Seek whatever is left—
> that is my advice. (V 95)

Even as Lallā's verses make references to Śiva as a male
deity, the underlying current of her experiences is best
represented by those verses that portray Śiva as the

transcendental reality which is beyond any anthropomorphic representation, a reality that goes beyond subject-object duality since it is the essential ground of both.

The difficult task that Lallā faces is how to represent this reality using language that always objectifies what it represents. Also, any attempt to describe the metaphysical reality that exists outside the linguistic and epistemological structures of a culture is already influenced by the thought structures and language of the culture that attempts to describe it. Finally, she describes this state by simply saying what it is not. Lallā speaks about this final state in terms of nothingness coming in touch with nothingness.

> Neither you nor I
> and neither meditation
> nor the object of meditation exist.
> The All-doer forgets Himself.
> The blind find this meaningless.
> The wise become one
> with this supreme state. (V 61)

In yet another formulation of this concept, Lallā describes the sun as illuminating the world of objects. The setting of the sun, then, represents an introspective state when the individual withdraws attention from the objective sphere and rests in the subjective sphere. This state is compared to the shining of the moon. As the moon vanishes or as the practitioner goes beyond the subjective sphere, he experiences *śūnya* or nothingness.

> The sun sets,
> the moon shines.
> The moon vanishes,
> consciousness remains.
> Consciousness disappears,
> nothingness remains—
> the physical, spiritual, and metaphysical
> merge into nothingness. (V 31)

The sun and the moon in this verse refer to the practice that involves the control of vital breath and its ascent through the psychic centers. The setting of the sun and the moon represents two currents, *prāṇa* (*sūrya* or sun) and *apāna* (*candra* or moon) that join in the middle channel (*suṣumnā*), as the vital breath ascends upwards and develops into the concentrated point and on to the half moon, then breaking through the limit (*nirodhikā*), and on to yet subtler levels of awareness where the universal subjectivity predominates. In the *Spandakārikās*, similar verses appear:

> Once entered that state which (the yogi) takes as his support and firmly resolves that: 'I will surely do whatever He [Śiva] says,' both the sun and moon set, following the ascending way, into the channel of suṣumnā, once abandoned the sphere of the universe … Then in that great sky, when the sun and moon dissolve away, the dull minded (yogi is cast down) into a state like that of deep sleep. The awakened however remains lucid [V 23, 24, 25]. (*The Stanzas* xvi)

As the individual reaches higher states of awareness, Lallā says, it is possible to let go of this subjective sphere and experience a state when all dualities are transcended so that the physical, spiritual, and the metaphysical all come together in the experience of the new state.

Lallā also occasionally describes the process of realizing the highest state in terms of crossing six forests or six paths and seizing the seventh. The "six paths" refers to six cakras or energy centers along the spine— *mūlādhāra, svādhiṣṭhāna, maṇipura, anāhata, viśuddhā, ājñā*. The orb of the moon is the seventh cakra or *brahmarandhra*. The references once again are to the practices mentioned above and the ultimate goal is always to realize the state of nothingness or non-being, which Lallā refers to as "the abode of light."

After traversing six forests,
I awakened the orb of the moon.

> By controlling my breath,
> I gave up attachment to worldly things.
> I roasted my heart
> in the fire of love—
> I found Śankara that way. (V 67)

> I became absorbed in the sacred syllable Oṃ.
> I burned myself like coal.
> Leaving behind six paths,
> I seized the seventh—
> and then, I, Lallā, reached the abode of light. (V 28)

The *Svacchandatantra* discusses the development of the syllable Oṃ in terms of crossing seven voids, the first six of which are unstable because of vibration and hence, must be transcended in order to arrive at the seventh which, free of all states, is the highest void and represents "non-being." Thus, "Non-being is beyond contemplation, and its domain is beyond the universe; free of the mind, intellect and the rest, it is devoid of reason and doctrine. It is the imperishable Lord, beyond perception and the other means of knowledge, beyond all reason and authority, free of bondage and Mantra, omniscient, omnipresent, tranquil, pure, and free of limitations."[6] Lallā refers to the experience of "non-being" (*abhāva*) as nothingness (*śūnya*) in her verses not in negative or nihilistic terms, but more to represent a space that cannot be contained in any dualistic categories. Lallā's verses reflect her quest for transcendence. Her choice of images and metaphors, therefore, more often than not point toward creating disenchantment with worldly things. Her journey is a one-way journey to cross the river of life to reach the other shore. Even though Lallā embodies the state of detachment from the world and hence, possesses the ability to experience it in its fullness, yet there is a deliberate attempt on her part to stay locked out of any aesthetic experience of

---

[6] From the *Svacchandabhairavatantra*. Quoted in *The Stanzas* 211.

the world. The aesthetic delight that Abhinavagupta[7] writes
about in his work on poetry and drama is not available to
Lallā as she has turned away from the world. Her verses are
the only means through which she can manifest her joy and
creativity.

> I did not pause for the right moment.
> I did not trust anything.
> The wine I, Lallā, drank
> was my own verses.
> I caught the inner darkness,
> gathered it
> and tore it into shreds. (V 93)

Her most profound verses then reflect her desire to lose
herself in mystical experience rather than to use it as the
ground to lead a more fulfilling material existence. Thus,
she says,

> Impurities of my mind
> were wiped away as from a mirror,
> and I attained self-knowledge.
> I saw Him near me—
> He is everything,
> and I am nothing. (V 68)

---

[7] Abhinavagupta (10th century AD), a philosopher, literary critic, and
a great Shaivite teacher wrote extensively on the role of poetry and
drama to experience the bliss of the Self during moments of intense
emotional experiences when thought processes come to a complete
halt. Abhinava wrote two influential commentaries, the
Dhvanyālokalocana on the *Dhvanyāloka* of Ānandavardhana (9th century literary critic and poet), and the *Abhinavabhāratī* which expli-
cates the *Nāṭyaśāstra*, a work on dramaturgy by Bharata (500 AD). In
the *Abhinavabhāratī* while eulogizing poets, Abhinavagupta compares
the poet to the creator itself, because "the poet is endowed with a
power to create wondrous and unheard of things. This power arises
from the grace of *Parā Vāk* ("Highest Speech") which is just another
name for poetic imagination (*pratibhā*) which has its seat in the poet's
own heart, and which is eternally in creative motion (*udita*)" (quoted
in Masson 13).

Lallā justifies her renunciation of the world by describing it as an illusion, which is surprising considering the fact that she is a Śaiva practitioner. Kashmīrī Śaivites explicitly reject the position taken by nondualist Vedāntins that the world is an illusion or *māyā*. Nondualist Vedāntins believe that there is only one reality, which is transcendental and inactive Brahman. Once ignorance is removed, the world appears as what it actually is—Brahman. For example, in darkness it is easy to mistake a rope for a snake, but once light shines on the rope, the illusion is dispelled. Kashmīrī Śaivites, on the other hand, believe all manifest reality is real because it represents the unfolding of consciousness. The unfolding gives rise to diversity and infolding to withdrawal into the unity where the universe is held in a potential form. There are not two different moments or two different orders of reality here, but one moment with two aspects where one has the other implicit in it. Through the cultivation of the self as the Self, one realizes that the universal consciousness constitutes the ground of the three states of consciousness, deep sleep, dreaming, and waking, even as it abides in the fourth that transcends the three states. Śiva and Śakti, transcendence and immanence, represent two aspects of the same reality held together in a delicate balance, as each separately is only an incomplete description of reality.

Lallā comments upon the dynamism between Śiva and Śakti in terms of the interplay between the self (the finite consciousness) and Śiva or the Self (the universal consciousness). The realization of the Self within oneself, *ātmavyāpti,* and the realization of the Self as the substratum of the outside world, *śivavyāpti,* is the ultimate goal of her practice. The enlightened perspective reveals to her that the empirical and the universal, as well as the manifest and the unmanifest, are interwoven. The manifest world arises out of the womb of the unmanifest like waves arise from the ocean.

The efficacy of the notion of unity in duality or on a broader scale unity in multiplicity is closely related to what

perspective is used to describe the two aspects of reality that
are interwoven. The traditional interpretation of Śaivism has
been to regard liberation as the realization of an eternal
state that is changeless and timeless Absolute—the state of
Śiva consciousness. The aim of liberation, then, is to attain
to this state in order to escape from the ravages of time. For
example, the commentators of the *spanda* doctrine admit
that the ultimate consciousness and its vibration belong to
one moment rather than two different moments of reality,
even as they insist that ultimately Śiva is the eternal agent of
the cosmic process as well as individual experience.
Dyczkowski, however, writes that the original doctrine of
spanda did not make finer distinctions in its description of
the ultimate reality. In the *Spandakārikās*, in fact, there is
no contradiction seen in describing Śiva as both transcendent
and immanent in all states of consciousness and yet, whose
highest state of awareness transcends all states. According
to the *Spandakārikās*, Śiva

> is transcendentally immanent, with the stress being on
> His immanence as the experiencing subject (*bhoktṛ*)
> who, divested of all egoity, is not the individual soul
> (*puruṣa*) nor the individual perceiver (*grāhaka*) but his
> own personal fundamental state (*svasthiti*) or being
> (*svasvabhāva*). Engaged in the act of perception, he is
> also the pure agency (*kartṛtā*) which, although
> omniscient and omnipotent, is not centered on
> individual objects of perception or products of action,
> but is the universal underlying ground (*adhiṣṭhātṛ*) and
> activity (*sāmānyaspanda*)....Self realization is the
> astonishing insight into one's own fundamental state
> of being as Śiva in both domains of subjectivity and
> objectivity. (Dyczkowski *The Stanzas* 186)

The original *spanda* doctrine thus represents the middle
ground between the Śiva-oriented *pratyabhijñā* philosophy
and the Śakti-oriented *krama* system of Kashmīrī Śaivism.
The most empowering interpretation of Śaivism would be

to define liberation in terms of a process where self-realization is neither to be lost in the transcendent and restful Śiva nor to find oneself limited to the domain of Śakti.

Perhaps we can understand this concept better if we refer to recent discoveries in quantum mechanics, which cannot be explained on the basis of categories of human understanding and normal sense perceptions. At the quantum level the subatomic particles appear as both waves and particles. If instruments were used to describe their position, they would register as particles, and if their momentum was measured, they would appear as waves. Each by itself is thus an incomplete description of the subatomic reality. Both the wave and particle descriptions are needed to give the complete picture. More fundamentally, reality is potential. By exercising awareness in different ways, the many possibilities are reduced to specific actuality.

The evolution of phenomenal reality is contingent on the ground-stuff of consciousness. The well-known quantum physicist David Bohm proposes a theory of reality based on his synthesis of insights into quantum reality with Eastern philosophical ideas. Bohm theorizes that there is an implicate order enfolded in the entire universe, and at that level everything is interconnected and a part of the whole. Becoming and not being is the basis of reality. A Śaivite would say reality is the play of consciousness, and a physicist metaphysician might say reality is process—a flow of processes that are novel, creative, and evolving. Everything is part of the flux of this everchanging reality.

Both the Self and the self are intricately intertwined. No eternity exists apart from temporal existence—one is enfolded in the other and does not exist apart from the other. Śiva and Śakti are two aspects of the same indeterminate reality so that one can say that reality is both Śiva and Śakti. "The motion of absolute consciousness is a creative movement, a transition from the uncreated state of Being to the created state of Becoming. In this sense Being is in a state of perpetual Becoming ...it constantly phenomenalises into finite expression" (Dyczkowski 1987, 77).

Kashmīrī Śaivites describe the Self or Śiva as a painter who paints on the screen of his own consciousness or as an artist who brings forth the world for his own delight. The world is the result of the tāṇḍava dance of Śiva through which he expresses his pure joy and freedom. Since Śiva or the Self underlies both the self and the world, the ultimate aim of the individual is to become aware of one's true nature (*svasvabhāva*). To experience the world as the aesthetic expression of Śiva is compared in the Śaiva texts to the experience of an artwork. The highest art is not a realistic representation of the external world, but the expression of joy and freedom of the Self. Abhinavagupta says that for a reader or a spectator of an artistic work, "the enjoyment of an aesthetic experience consists of a transcendental wonder (*alaukikacamatkāra*) and is decidedly (*eva*) different from ordinary (*laukika*) knowledge such as (is produced) by memory and inference."[8] The poet uses creative imagination (*pratibhā*) to express the greatest freedom and joy of creation. Great poetry invokes in the reader feelings of awe and wonder, filling him with amazement (*camatkāra*). During such an experience the distance between the subject and object disappears. Time and space dissolve. The transcendence of the empirical ego leads to self-forgetfulness and total immersion in the moment.[9] Just as it is in the experience of art and poetry, so it can be in the experience

---

[8] Abhinavagupta in the *Abhinavabhāratī*. Quoted in Masson 48.

[9] In Towards a *Psychology of Being*, Abraham Maslow uses similar terminology to describe peak experiences, which are intense experience of creative, mystical, philosophical, and emotional nature. Peak experiences are the experiences of highest happiness and fulfillment. In this state perception transcends the ego and one experiences wonder, amazement, humility and even reverence. Maslow's description of peak experiences very well illustrates the Śaiva belief that intense experience of emotions, mystical or creative in nature, lead to the transcendence of the empirical ego and the experience of our Śiva nature.

of the world as the creative play of consciousness.

The need to play is intrinsic to reality—the play here means nature's tendency to create meaningful order out of diverse phenomena marked by creativity and novelty. Liberation, then, is the realization that the true nature of reality is becoming. The description of reality as the tāṇḍava dance of Śiva illustrates the process of becoming and hints at its creative and aesthetic elements. The *Śiva Sūtras* say: "The Self is the actor or the dancer (*nartaka ātmā*)" (*Aphorisms* 105). A good actor is sensitive to the emotive states (*rasa*) of the play and identifies completely with the part she plays and yet in between the scenes, she reverts back to her own self and rejoices in the play of creation. Similarly, the Self within the self acts out its world drama through the activity of the senses, taking delight in its unfolding in the diversity of the manifest reality. According to the *Spandakārikās* "the realization of the liberated condition is the achievement of a state of pure enjoying subjectivity (*bhoktṛtā*), through which perfect mastery of every power is acquired...The liberated yogi thus conforms to Śiva's state which, beyond the opposites of subject and object, pleasure and pain, is the subject who enjoys the cosmic sport of the cycle of His universal manifestation" (Dyczkowski, *The Stanzas* 186).

To say that Lallā actually read these texts would be to plunge into ahistoricism and deny her the specificity of the historical moment she occupies. Her worldview is very much shaped by the ideology of the medieval period. In spite of remarkable insights into the nature of reality she attains through her Śaivite practice, she can only experience these insights in a disembodied fashion, without integrating them into her lived reality. This in fact limits her potential to lead a fulfilling life at the physical level, even as she achieves an advanced state of awareness at the spiritual level.

In another work, *To the Other Shore: Lalla's Life and Poetry*, I argue that Lallā's asceticism was due to her location as a woman practitioner within the Kashmīrī Śaiva tradition. This location placed her spiritual attainment in a contradictory position to the traditional role of a woman and a wife in which self-effacement and subservience were promoted rather than self-mastery. Lallā's verses repeatedly point to the futility of observing religious practices that include asceticism and renunciation. In one of her verses, she says that even householders can achieve self-realization if they work hard at it. Her own life, however, contradicts the message in her teachings. Even as at one level, there is a need to transcend dualism, at another level her words are marked by the dualism of mind and body.

To bring out the relevance of Lallā's poetry for contemporary society, it is important to emphasize that the Kaśmīrī Śaivism which permeates her verses does not promote renunciation of the world. The *Spandakārikās* describe the relationship of the Self and the world as that between the mirror and its reflection. The reflection is not something separate from the mirror, just as the created world is not separate from the Self. However, unlike the reflection, which is of an object outside the mirror, there is nothing outside the consciousness that gets reflected. This is an important distinction, which illustrates that the relationship between the consciousness and the empirical world is not based on positing the world as the other, outside of itself, and thereby assigning it a different order of reality. Instead, the empirical world exists within the mirror of consciousness and hence, the two are integrally related. The world is not a negative image of the Self. In order to experience the Self, one need not negate the world since it is an expression of the Self. Once the enlightened perspective is achieved, the world can be enjoyed as the creative manifestation of the universal consciousness.

In Lallā's verses, in spite of their Śaiva content, there is an undue stress on the mirror part of the above metaphor, and it is a mirror that does not reflect the world. The light of consciousness that illumines her inner reality bounces off the social structures of her material reality. Lallā's dancing is not the dancing of Śiva taking delight in his creation. Her

life experiences in fact deconstruct the metaphor of dance—
she symbolically divests herself of the body that would enable
her to enjoy the dance. For her, the world is indeed *māyā,*
which hinders rather than helps her enjoy her insights into
reality.

(Adapted from Chapters 4 & 5 of Jaishree Kak Odin's
To the Other Shore: Lalla's Life and Poetry, Vitasta Pub,
1999.)

Concordance of Various Lallā Collections

Kak	Grierson	A. Koul	Koshur Samāchār	J. Kaul/ Kotru	Parimoo
1	98		2	5	16
2	106		1	1	4
3		13 (1930)	6	14	15
4	41		10	8	19
5	67		5	2	14
6	108		3	23	24
7		12 (1930)	4	4	17
8		13 (1932)	54k	43	
9		13 (1932)	54 kh	42	23
10	83		87	9	2
11	18		57	39	6
12	8		46	73	12
13	102		115 k	105	
14	103		115kh	105	
15	7		75	129	20
16	95		8	6	60
17	13		114	128	21
18		12 (1932)	81	75	
19	105		82	88	35
20		11 (1932)	56		
21		15 (1933)	63	25	11
22		5 (1931)	13	24	26
23	48		34	74	32
24	109		131	127	64
25	56			95	67
26	57		141	96	68
27	101		20		31
28	82		127	94	53

Kak	Grierson	A. Koul	Koshur Samāchār	J. Kaul/ Kotru	Parimoo
29	69		21	91	42
30		1 (1931)	122		
31	9		107	85	45
32	44		132	136	50
33		9 (1930)	116	125	98
34		24 (1932)	31	126	
35		19 (1932)	118	103	100
36	42		125	70	57
37		10 (1931)	29	87	
38		16 (1932)	53	47	92
39	93		133	137	101
40	96		85	10	
41	3		36	97	
42		17 (1932)	52	46	90
43	58		134	138	
44	49		35	86	37
45		12 (1933)	112	131	
46	4		27	98	33
47	76		129	102	97
48	6		79	118	52
49		25 (1930)	48	44	
50	94		14	21	27
51		3 (1930)		116	
52	97		86	11	
53	33		124	71	54
54	78		95	119	69
55	79		96	120	70
56	14		97	121	65
57	15		98	122	66
58		20 (1932)	25	63	34
59	26		23	52	30
60	1		108	133	39
61	59		110	135	47
62	22			117	49

Kak	Grierson	A. Koul	Koshur Samāchār	J. Kaul/ Kotru	Parimoo
63	16		111	83	48
64	24		68	64	
65	60		37	99	46
66	84				18
67	25		83	93	38
68	31		130	100	51
69	68		121	130	44
70	81			115	
71	87			17	
72	107		16	15	
73	23			41	
74	32		91	111	87
75	72		40	29	22
76	28		60	33	81
77		7 (1931)	64	27	80
78	27		65	30	
79	34		26	72	28
80	38		69	112	88A
81	64		78	109	77
82	5		74	132	74
83		21 (1932)	105	57	
84	61		12	49	85
85	75			101	96
86	54		101		
87		17 (1930)	67k	54	
88		17 (1930)	67kh	55	
89		27 (1932)	30	20	
90		11 (1933)	28	28	5
91	43		70	36	83
92	65		76	110	75
93	104			92	
94		5 (1930)	120	26	3
95	2		109	134	40
96	11		106	89	41

Kak	Grierson	A. Koul	Koshur Samāchār	J. Kaul/ Kotru	Parimoo
97		6 (1930)	135		73
98	55		77	108	76
99	45		43	67	56
100		16 (1930)	113	123	
101	21		55	38	7
102	29		38	76	36
103		10 (1930)	92	56	
104	51		99	77	
105	19		11	7	78
106	50		94	114	58
107	35		123	104	
108	47		93	113	59
109		20 (1930)	80		
110		20 (1930)	80		
111	17		41	66	55
112		3 (1933)	32	50	
113		23 (1932)	7	3	
114	74			13	95
115		32 (1930)	157-158	18	9
116	36		45	107	62
117		4 (1930)	51	45	91
118		10 (1933)	62	34	
119	37		22	51	84
120	62		15	22	25
121		14 (1932)	119	58	
122	80		24	80	29
123	39		42k	68	71
124	40		42kh	69	72
125	30		73	90	43
126	52		100	78	
127	66		50	16	
128	53		102	79	
129	88		33	35	
130		23 (1930)	39	59	

Kak	Grierson	A. Koul	Koshur Samāchār	J. Kaul/ Kotru	Parimoo
131	63		17	62	63
132		19 (1930)	44	65	93
133	12		66	48	86
134	71		71	37	82
135	20		58	40	10
136	10		154	61	13
137		7 (1930)	156	19	
138	77			60	
139		6 (1931)	59	31	
140		6 (1931)	59	32	
141	70			53	79
142	73			12	94
143	86			106	
144	46		104	84	61
145		31 (1930)	103	82	
146		28 (1930)	72	124	

Bibliography

Translations and Commentaries of Lallā's Verses

Kaul, Jayalal. *Lal Ded*. New Delhi: Sahitya Akademi, 1973.

Koshur Samāchār: A Socio-Cultural Monthly. Lalded Number. Vol. IX, No.1 (Jan.-Feb. 1971), pp. 1-58.

Koul, Pandit Ananda. "Life Sketch of Laleshwari" and "Lallā-Vākyāni." *The Indian Antiquary*. Vols. L (1921), pp. 309-12; LIX (1930), pp. 108-30; LX (1931), pp. 191-93; LXI (1932), pp. 13-16; LXII (1933), pp.108-11.

Lal Ded: Her Life and Sayings. Trans., Nil Kanth Kotru. Srinagar: Utpal Publications, 1989.

Lallā-Vākyāni: or The Wise Sayings of Lal Ded. Ed. and trans., Sir George Grierson and ·Lionell D. Barnett. London: Royal Asiatic Society, 1920.

Lalleśvari: Lallayogeśvari kī vānī. Trans., Svāmī Muktānand Paramahaṃsa. Ganeśpurī, Mahārāṣṭra: Srī Gurudeva Ashrama, 1972.

Naked Song. Trans., Coleman Barks. Athens, GA: Maypole Pub, 1992.

Odin, Jaishree Kak. *To the Other Shore: Lalla's Life and Poetry*. New Delhi: Vitasta, 1999.

Parimoo, B.N. *The Ascent of Self.* 2nd edn. Delhi: Motilal Banarsidass, 1987.

Temple, Richard Carnac. *The Religion and Teachings of Lalla*. New Delhi: Vintage Books, 1990.

The Wise Sayings of Laleshwari. Trans., S.N. Charagi. Srinagar: Trust Publishing House, 1938.

Related Works on Aesthetics, Poetry, Philosophy, Religion, and History

The Aphorisms of Śiva with a Commentary by Bhāskaracārya, the Vārttika. Trans., Mark S. G. Dyczkowski. Varanasi, India: Dilip Kumar Publishers, 1991.

Bailly, Constantina R. *Shaiva Devotional Songs of Kashmir: A Translation and Study of Utpaladeva's Shivastotravali*. Albany, NY: SUNY Press, 1987.

Bamzai, Prithivi N. K. *A History of Kashmir*. Delhi: Metropolitan Book Co, 1962.

Bazaz, P.N. *Daughters of the Vitasta*.New Delhi: Pamposh Publications, 1959.

Bhagavad Gītā. Trans. Sri Swami Śivānanda. Durban: Sivānanda Press, 1983.

Bohm, David. *Wholeness and the Implicate Order*. London: Routledge and Kegan Paul, 1980.

Chatterji, J. C. *Kashmir Shaivism*. Albany, NY: SUNY Press, 1982.

Dhar, Triloki Nath. *Rūpa Bhawāni: Life, Teachings, and Philosophy*. Srinagar: Valley Printing Press, 1977.

The Dhvanyāloka of Ānandavardhana. With the *Locana* of Abhinavagupta. Trans., Daniel H. H. Ingalls, Jeffrey M. Masson and M.V. Patwardhan. Massachusetts: Harvard University Press, 1990.

Dhvanyāloka of Ānandavardhana. Ed. And·Trans., K. Krishnamoorthy. Delhi: Motilal Banarsidass, 1974.

Drabu, Vishva Nath. *Śaivāgamas*. New Delhi: Indus Publishing Company, 1990.

Ä Dyczkowski, Mark S. G. *The Doctrine of Vibration: An Analysis of the Doctrines and Practices of Kashmir Shaivism*. New York: SUNY press, 1987.

Flood, Gavin. *Body and Cosmology in Kashmir Śaivism*. San Francisco: Mellon Research University Press, 1993.

Gnoli, Raniero. *The Aesthetic Experience According to Abhinavagupta*. Varanasi: Chowkhamba Sanskrit Series, 1985.

Hasan, Mohibbul. *Kashmir under the Sultans*. Calcutta, India: Iran Society, 1959.

Hughes, John. *Self Realization in Kashmir Shaivism: The Oral Teachings of Swami Lakshmanjoo*. New York: SUNY Press, 1995.

Jonarāja. *Rājataraṅgiṇī of Jonarāja*. Trans., Jogesh Chunder Dutt. Delhi: Gian Publishing House, 1986.

Kachru, Braj B. *Kashmiri Literature*. Wiesbaden: Otto Harrassowitz, 1981.

Kak, Ram Nath. *Autumn Leaves*. New Delhi: Vitasta Publications, 1996.

Kak, Subhash C. "On the Science of Consciousness in Ancient India." *Indian Journal of History of Science*, 32 (2), 1997.

Kalahana. *Rājataraṅgiṇī*. Trans., R.S. Pandit. New Delhi: Sahitya Akademi, 1990.

Kalhana. *Rājataraṅgiṇī*. Trans. M.A. Stein. Vols I & II. Delhi: Motilal Banarsidass, 1961.

Knowles, James Hinton. *A Dictionary of Kashmiri Proverbs & Sayings*. Reprint of 1885 edn. New Delhi : Asian Educational Services, 1985.

Kramrisch, Stella. *The Presence of Śiva*. Princeton, N.J.: Princeton University Press, 1981.

Kṣemarāja. "The Essence of Vibration, the SpandaSamdoha" in *The Stanzas on Vibration: The Spandakārikās with Four Commentaries*. Trans., Mark S. G. Dyczkowski. New York: SUNY Press, 1992. Pp. 61-72.

Kumar, Pushpendra. *Śakti Cult in Ancient India*. Varanasi: Bhartiya Publishing House, 1974.

Lakshman Jee, Swami. *Kashmir Shaivism: The Secret Supreme*. New York: SUNY Press,1988.

Lakshman Jee, Swami. *Shiva Sutras: The Supreme Awakening*. Ed. John Hughes. USA: Authorhouse, 2002.

Madan, T.N. *Family and Kinship: A Study of the Pandits of Rural Kashmir*. Delhi: Oxford University Press, 1989.

Maslow, Abraham H. *Toward a Psychology of Being.* Princeton, N.J.: Van Nostrand, 1968.

Masson, J.L. and M.V. Patwardhan. *Śāntarasa and Abhinavagupta's Philosophy of Aesthetics.* Reprint of 1969 edition. Poona: Bhandarkar Oriental Research Institute, 1985.

Mishra, Kamalkar. *Kashmir Śaivism: The Central Philosophy of Tantrism.* Rudra Press: Cambridge, Ma, 1993.

Muktananda, Swami. *Nothing Exists That Is Not Shiva: Commentaries on the Shiva Sutra, Vijñāna Bhairava, Guru Gita and Other Sacred Texts.* Siddha Yoga Publications, 1997.

Muktananda, Swami. *Play of Consciousness.* San Francisco: Harper and Row, 1978.

Muller-Ortega, Paul Eduardo. *The Triadic Heart of Śiva.* Albany, NY: SUNY Press, 1989.

O'Flaherty, Wendy Doniger. *Asceticism and Eroticism in the Mythology of Śiva.* London: Oxford University Press, 1973.

Pandey, K. C. *Comparative Aesthetics.* Vol. I. Varanasi: Chowkhamba Sanskrit Series Office, 1959.

Pandit, B. N. *Aspects of Kashmir Śaivism.* Srinagar: Utpal Publication. 1977.

Pandit, B. N. *History of Kashmir Śaivism.* Srinagar: Utpal Publication, 1990.

Pratyabhijñānhṛdyam: The Secret of Self Recognition. Trans., Jaideva Singh. Delhi: Motilal Banarsidass, 1979.

Rafiqi, Abdul Qaiyum. *Sufism in Kashmir.* Varanasi, Delhi, India: Bharatiya Publishing House, 1972.

Rastogi, Navjivan. *The Krama Tantricism of Kashmir.* Vol. I. Delhi: Motilal Banarsidass, 1979.

Ramanujan, A. K. *Speaking of Shiva.* Maryland, U.S.A.: Penguin, 1973.

Ray, S. C. *Early History and Culture in Kashmir.* Delhi, India: Motilal Banarsidass, 1969.

Sangari, Kumkum. "Mirabai and the Spiritual Economy of *Bhakti*" *Economic and Political Weekly*. July 7, 1990.

Silburn, Lilian. *Kuṇḍalinī: The Energy of the Depths*. Trans. Jacques Gontier. New York: State University of New York, 1988.

Sastri, P.S. *Indian Theory of Aesthetics*. Delhi: Bharariya Vidya Prakashan, 1989.

Shrīvara's *Jainarājataraṅgiṇī* in *Medieval Kashmir*. Ed. S. L. Sadhu. Reprint of the J. C. Dutta's translation of *Rājtaraṅgiṇīs* of Jonarāja, Shrīvara and Shuka (published in 1898 AD under the title *Kings of Kashmira* Vol III). New Delhi, India: Atlantic Publishers, 1993.

The Śiva Purāna. Vols. 1-4. Ed., J. L. Shastri. Delhi: Motilal Banarsidass, 1995.

Śiva Sūtras: The Yoga of Supreme Identity. Trans., Jaideva Singh. Delhi: Motilal Banarsidass, 1979.

Spanda Kārikās. Trans. Jaideva Singh. Delhi: Motilal Banarsidass, 1980.

The Stanzas on Vibration: The Spandakārikās with Four Commentaries. Trans, Mark S. G. Dyczkowski. New York: SUNY Press, 1992.

Sūfī, G.M.D. *Kashīr: A History of Kashmir*. Vols. 1 & 2. New Delhi: Light and Life Publishers, 1974.

Swamy, H. Thipperudra. *The Viraśaiva Saints: A Study*. Trans. S. M. Angadi. Mysore, India: Rao and Raghavan, 1968.

Vijñānabhairava or Divine Consciousness. Trans. Jaideva Singh. Delhi: Motilal Banarsidass, 1979.

Walimbe, Y.S. *Abhinavagupta on Indian Aesthetics*. Delhi: Ajanta Publications, 1980.

Woodroffe, John. *Śakti and Śākta*. Madras: Ganesh and Company, 1987.

Index